LANDMARK LAW CASES

&

AMERICAN SOCIETY

Peter Charles Hoffer
N. E. H. Hull
Series Editors

DAVID M. O'BRIEN

Animal Sacrifice and Religious Freedom

Church of the Lukumi Babalu Aye

v. City of Hialeah

UNIVERSITY PRESS OF KANSAS

Published by the University Press of Kansas (Lawrence, Kansas 66049), which was
organized by the Kansas Board of Regents and is operated and funded by
Emporia State University, Fort Hays State University, Kansas State University,
Pittsburg State University, the University of Kansas, and Wichita State University

Library of Congress Cataloging-in-Publication Data

O'Brien, David M.
Animal sacrifice and religious freedom : Church of the Lukumi Babalu
Aye v. City of Hialeah / David M. O'Brien.
p.   cm. — (Landmark law cases & American society)
Includes bibliographical references and index.
ISBN 0-7006-1302-1 (cloth : alk. paper) — ISBN 0-7006-1303-x (pbk. :
alk. paper)
1. Church of the Lukumi Babalu Aye (Hialeah, Fla.) — Trials,
litigation, etc.   2. Hialeah (Fla.) — Trials, litigation, etc.   3.
Religious minorities — Legal status, laws, etc. — United States.   4.
Animal sacrifice — Law and legislation — United States.   5. Freedom of
religion — United States.   I. Title.   II. Series.
KF228.c498O25   2004
342.7308'52—DC22   2003023966
British Library Cataloguing-in-Publication Data is available.

Printed in the United States of America

10 9 8 7 6 5 4 3 2 1

The paper used in this publication meets the minimum requirements of the
American National Standard for Permanence of Paper for Printed Library Materials
z39.48-1984.

For Claudine and our three
wonderful children: Benjamin,
Sara, and Talia

CONTENTS

Animal Sacrifice and Religious Freedom is a riveting account of a freedom of worship case with more twists and turns, bizarre subplots, and eccentric characters than a classic whodunit. The outline of the story seems clear enough. Ernesto Pichardo, a Cuban immigrant in the 1960s and a self-styled priest of Santeria, sets up a new church in Florida. The sect is an old one, fusing Afro-Cuban ancestor worship, African rituals, and Roman Catholic saints, but Pichardo's version of it emphasizes its African religious roots and universal truths. Central to these are ritual sacrifices of animals to propitiate the *orishas*, African ancestral deities. But Pichardo is not of African ancestry, and from its inception his church faces criticism from other adherents of Santeria, the Cuban community, and animal rights advocates.

Enter the convoluted and perhaps corrupt politics of the Florida city of Hialeah, where Pichardo tries to turn a former used-car dealership into a church. Add to this a cast of local and state politicians who have their own agendas, fiercely committed humane society spokespeople, lawyers for the local chapter of the American Civil Liberties Union (ACLU), a liberal Texas law professor who argues the case for Pichardo on the grounds of modern doctrines of tolerance for minorities, a conservative law professor from Utah who argues the case for Pichardo on the grounds of biblical traditions of animal sacrifice, and a cast of dozens of expert witnesses on everything from child psychology to the proper way to slaughter chickens, and the plot thickens. The city passes ordinances against the ritual sacrifice of animals that look general but are clearly aimed at Pichardo's Church of the Lukumi Babalu Aye. Pichardo protests in vain that he and his followers are being persecuted, and he sues in federal court. A federal judge rules for the city, finding that the new church's rituals are not humane, that the disposal of the carcasses poses a health risk, and that the entire rite is harmful to children. A panel of the circuit court of appeals concurs. But the story is not over.

Against all odds, the Supreme Court of the United States agrees to hear Pichardo's appeal. The high court's First Amendment jurisprudence is in disarray. In its decisions, the free exercise clause of the amendment seems to run head-on into the establishment clause. The Court's ruling in a recent Oregon case has raised some of the same issues as Pichardo's appeal and has set the Court against Congress, the mainstream faiths, and much of the nation. The ACLU, a variety of religious groups, the Humane Society of the United States, the city of Hialeah, and the state of Florida square off in oral arguments before the justices. The stage is set for one of the most fascinating and momentous freedom of worship cases in the twentieth century. How will the Court rule? And how will its members justify their positions?

In this lively and swift-paced narrative, David M. O'Brien, one of our country's leading students of the Supreme Court, unravels all these mysteries. He takes us behind the scenes at every stage of the litigation, introduces us to the remarkable cast of characters, and probes the motives behind their words and deeds. He introduces us to African worship practices, the politics of Hialeah municipal government, the origins of animal rights, and the way the U.S. Supreme Court goes about its business. The technical legal argument becomes a conversation in which we, vicariously, take part. That conversation ranges widely, from discussions of primitive magical acts to the most arcane points in constitutional law.

But the case is more than one moment in an ongoing debate over the rights of religious sects, and this book is more than just a gripping story well told. Ernesto Pichardo's effort to gain for himself and his followers the right to conduct services in a house of worship touches on two issues of great importance. Our courts had reaffirmed the constitutional principle that the freedom of religious belief is absolute, but they had held that the freedom to practice the tenets of any faith is subject to the regulations of the state. In *Church of the Lukumi Babalu Aye, Inc., and Ernesto Pichardo v. City of Hialeah*, Pichardo and his congregation won the right to practice what they believed, as well as to talk about it. What was more, they proved that even the least of us, a newcomer with few resources whose opinions were far from the mainstream, could gain a day in the highest court of the land.

ACKNOWLEDGMENTS

This book combines legal history with political anthropology in a study of the politics of interest-group litigation and the Supreme Court. Its completion would not have been possible without the support and encouragement of friends, colleagues, and many others. When the case was argued in the Supreme Court, I used it for a moot court in my undergraduate course on civil rights and civil liberties at the University of Virginia, and the students found it fascinating. At the time, I was working on a book on religious minorities in Japan, *To Dream of Dreams: Religious Freedom and Constitutional Politics in Postwar Japan*, which added to my interest in the case. Years later, I was invited to a series of conferences at Florida International University in Miami. As a result of those visits, I became committed to further researching the case, and my colleagues at Florida International University made it possible for me to spend a semester there in 2002. I therefore owe a special debt to John F. Stack Jr., director of the Jack Gordon Center for Public Policy, and Nicol Rae, chair of the Department of Political Science. Others there were also supportive in various ways, including Colton C. Campbell, Rebecca Mae Salokar, and Isabel Castellanos. Mary Volcansek, who has since gone on to a deanship elsewhere, deserves my appreciation as well.

Interviews with a number of individuals involved with the case proved most helpful. Although some of them may disagree with my assessments and interpretation, I appreciate their taking the time to assist me and absolve them of any responsibility for mistakes. Ernesto Pichardo, a cofounder of the Church of the Lukumi Babalu Aye and a principal in the suit against the city of Hialeah, generously spent time with me, as did his attorney, Jorge A. Duarte. University of Texas Law School professor Douglas Laycock, who argued the case in the Court of Appeals for the Eleventh Circuit and in the Supreme Court, also kindly talked with me about his involvement. So, too, did Richard G. Garrett, the lead attorney who represented the city of Hialeah in the trial and appellate court, as well as before the Supreme Court. I also benefited from conversations with Georgetown University professor of religious studies Joseph Murphy.

Part of the book was delivered as lectures at the Universite Lumiere

Lyon 2, in France, and as the Gould Lecture at the University of Vermont. I benefited from comments and discussions on those occasions and am particularly indebted to Professors Vincent Michelot, Jean Kempf, A. E. Dick Howard, Marci Hamilton, and Lisa M. Holmes, as well as Stephen Shapiro of the American Civil Liberties Union.

Others who deserve mention include the librarian of the Supreme Court, Shelley Dowling. Vanessa Yarnall, in the Office of the Administrative Assistant to the Chief Justice, a good friend for over twenty years, was supportive even if cynically amused by the project. Professors Peter Charles Hoffer and N. E. H. Hull kindly agreed to include the book in their series Landmark Law Cases and American Society, for which I am appreciative. Linda J. Lotz did a terrific job copyediting the manuscript. Finally, Michael Briggs and Fred M. Woodward made working on the book with the University Press of Kansas enjoyable.

Last but not least, as always I am grateful to my wife, Claudine, and our three wonderful children — Benjamin, Sara, and Talia. They put up with my travels and writing with their usual understanding and support. Even though they, along with a number of colleagues, found the project a bit strange, I could not have completed it without them.

CHAPTER I

Of Memories and Dreams

Born in 1954, Ernesto Pichardo was among the first major wave of Cuban immigrants to land on the shores of the United States, escaping Fidel Castro's grip after the 1959 revolution. Like other immigrants from around the world, his family sought freedom — freedom from repression, imprisonment, and even death for their beliefs. He became a citizen and eventually spearheaded a fight for religious freedom that went all the way to the Supreme Court.

One day in Cuba, recalls Pichardo, his teacher came home with him after school. She told his mother, Carmen Pla, that her son and other young men would be sent to Russia. There, he would learn Russian, train in the military, and be indoctrinated into communism. His mother immediately decided that he should not go back to school. They would escape. Before the revolution, she had traveled frequently to Florida and New York to buy jewelry for a business and later for a store in Havana's Hilton Hotel. Havana had once been bustling with nightclubs, casinos, and international travelers. Her family, though not wealthy, had lived a comfortable upper-middle-class life. After the revolution, life changed dramatically for them and for all Cubans, regardless of whether they stayed or fled.

Pichardo's family had long opposed communism. Back in the 1920s, his grandfather had a radio show on which he spoke out against communism. His mother was deeply religious, a devoted spiritualist. At the age of three she experienced her first incantation. In the 1930s, she was initiated into Palo Monte, an Afro-Cuban religion. A young servant-cook in her house initiated her and oversaw her spiritual development. Palo Monte and other Afro-Cuban religions such as Lukumi-Yoruba are rooted in the ancient religious practices of tribes from what is now Nigeria and western Africa. In Cuba, many followers of Palo Monte and Lukumi also identify with Catholicism and Espiritismo. In the

1940s, Carmen Pla was initiated into Espiritismo — at the time a popular form of spiritualism among members of the white middle and upper classes for invoking spirits through clairvoyants and séances. Although she continued to conduct Espiritismo séances and initiations, in 1970, almost a decade after arriving in the United States, she became a priestess *(iyalosha)* in the Lukumi religion as well.

Carmen Pla had no doubts about fleeing communist Cuba. Through séances she knew that the country was in trouble. So after the 1961 Bay of Pigs invasion by anti-Castro forces backed by the Central Intelligence Agency (CIA), Carmen and Raul Rodriguez, who became Pichardo's stepfather, escaped. Pichardo's father remained in Cuba. Castro's government already had Carmen on a list of people wanted for questioning, but under her name as an *espiritist*. Fortunately, she had used her real name on the passport.

Ernesto Pichardo and his brother Fernando, five years older, stayed behind with their grandparents. A month later, they were on their way to the airport to join their mother in America, but their grandfather and the driver felt that something was not right, so they turned back. A couple of days later, they tried again. This time, they made it to the airport. The boys' grandfather pointed out a flight attendant and told them to stick with her until they saw their mother inside the Miami airport.

After landing, Pichardo remembers looking for his mother behind a huge glass wall. A shouting crowd was waiting for their relatives to arrive. Inside the terminal, the boys were reunited with their mother, and the flight attendant disappeared.

Life was different but not easier in Miami. They moved into what became known as Little Havana. Initially, they lived in a small wooden tool shed in the backyard of a property owned by an Italian American who rented out several apartments behind his house. He converted a shack into a place for them to live, but it remained rat and roach invested.

With little money, Pichardo's mother sold her gold jewelry when emergencies arose. His stepfather, who had earned several college degrees in Cuba, woke at five in the morning and walked the streets of Little Havana looking for work. He did all sorts of odd jobs. Finally, he got his first real job from a manager Carmen Pla had met on an earlier business trip to Miami. It consisted of cleaning ashtrays and bathrooms and polishing chrome at the grand Eden Roc Hotel in Miami Beach. Soon he began parking cars there for tips, and he continued to take other part-time jobs as well. Carmen Pla eventually got a job as a seamstress at a garment manufacturing company supplying Macy's in New York. Years later, she and a distant cousin started their own small garment business. Through it all, she continued to conduct séances and other rites.

During these early years, Ernesto and Fernando Pichardo were largely left alone. They would wake up, eat breakfast, do laundry, and wash before walking to school. On Sundays, they went to Catholic services, where Ernesto was an altar boy. Like most who arrived shortly after the Cuban revolution, they had left their comfortable middle-class lives behind. They began their new lives in the turbulent 1960s and 1970s in a country in the midst of the Cold War and torn by struggles over civil rights and the war in Vietnam.

In these and other ways, Pichardo's story was similar to that of other immigrants; yet in other ways, it was not. Like most of the Cubans arriving in the early 1960s, his family was white; less than 5 percent arriving then were black or nonwhite Cubans. Still, they were strangers in a strange land. In Little Havana, he and his brother soon identified with their mother's spiritual beliefs and practices, known as Santeria.

Lukumi-Santeria is rooted in the ancient religious practices of the Lukumi, the people from Yorubaland. How their centuries-old religious practices became known as Santeria is part of the history of African slaves brought to Cuba and elsewhere in the New World.

Out of Africa

The Lukumi-Yoruba people are culturally diverse, once embracing more than 250 different ethnic groups. Only in the last century and a half did they became known as Lukumi, from the Yoruba *Omo Ife*, "children of Ife." Ife is believed to be the spot where the world was created, the Yoruba Garden of Eden. Ife was the royal city of a hereditary kingship governing one of Africa's first urban people. Ife, however, was only one of twenty-nine principalities in which different dialects were spoken and different traditions and customs observed.

The term *Yoruba* once applied only to the Oyo people who lived north of Ife. In the late 1600s, Oyo was the capital of an empire under the king *(oba)* of Oyo. In the eighteenth and nineteenth centuries, Yorubaland was racked by wars. With the disintegration of the kingdom came the expansion of tribal slavery and trading in slaves with Europeans. In 1808, England outlawed the slave trade and the exportation of African peoples. In subsequent decades, the British repatriated Africans freed from captured slave ships — many of whom were Oyo — taking them to the colony of Sierra Leone. Still, the slave trade continued into the 1860s in Yoruba territories and led to further colonial intervention. By 1900, all of Yorubaland, including the surrounding tribes and cultures, was a subject of Queen Victoria's British Empire. In 1914, the boundaries of modern Nigeria were established, and the country remained under British control until 1960, when Nigeria finally became an independent nation.

One of the repatriated Oyos in the early nineteenth century was the Reverend Samuel Crowther. He produced the first dictionary of the Yoruba language, written in his dialect of Oyo. It became the standard used by colonial officials. In time, Lukumi-Yoruba became the standard for the spoken language and was applied to all people who spoke any related dialect.

As in other African cultures, Yoruba life was organized based on lineage, including the living — immediate and extended families — the dead, and unborn generations. The Yoruba worshipped Olodumare ("owner of heaven," "owner of all destinies") and the incarnation of *ashe* ("cosmic blood or current of life and the universe"). *Orishas* — spirits or guardians — are personifications of the *ashe*. They are worshipped in temples as "the people of heaven" *(ara orun)*. Some, like Obatala, are direct emanations of Olodumare from heaven, who subsequently disappeared and turned to stone. Other *orishas* are worshipped for dying remarkable deaths or possessing special powers and knowledge. Among the hundreds of *orishas* worshipped is Oggun, the patron of smiths who can unlock earthly secrets and turn them into tools. Oshun represents the cooling *ashe* of rivers and brings health to her children. Among several widely worshipped *orishas* in Cuba, Nigeria, and elsewhere is Shango, once connected to the royal house of Oyo and symbol of the *ashe* of lightning, fire, and force. Alongside a pantheon of *orishas* are an individual's immediate ancestors and the founder of his or her community, who receive separate veneration.

The *orishas* are guardians and explicators of human destiny who provide instruction in how to grow in *ashe*. They are divine patrons and may be brought to the disposal of humans by priests and priestesses through divination, invocation, and proper care and feeding. One of the most important paths is that of *Ifa*, divination revealing one's destiny — revealing order amid the chaos and uncertainty of life. *Ifa* is also the name of the masters of divination, or "fathers of mystery," priests and priestesses who know the secret rites for invoking the *orishas*.

The Lukumi's rituals were preserved but transformed in the oral traditions of the slaves brought to Brazil, Cuba, and other parts of the Caribbean. By the time slavery ended in Brazil in 1888, an estimated 10 million Africans, many from Yorubaland, had been forced to take "the middle passage" to the New World. Estimates of those taken to Cuba range from 700,000 to more than a million. For a time in the nineteenth century, they accounted for 60 percent of the island's population and constituted the largest concentration of Lukumi-Yoruba outside of Africa.

———

In Cuba

The Cuba to which the Lukumi-Yoruba slaves were brought was ruled by Spain and dominated by the Roman Catholic Church. Several waves of slaves actually came to the island. The first wave began after the Spanish conquest of the island and continued for seventy-five years, with most slaves being brought to work in the sugar mills. The second wave began in the 1760s and lasted throughout most of the nineteenth century, during which staggering numbers arrived and were forced to work on plantations.

In the latter period, from about 1760 to the 1860s, the Catholic Church made a concerted effort to influence the religious practices of Cuba's African population. As Professor George Brandon emphasizes in his book *Santeria from Africa to the New World*, this was the "formative period" of what became known as the Lukumi religion or Santeria. From about 1870 to the Cuban revolution was a "transformative period," during which Santeria assumed "the form of a predominantly Yoruba-Spiritualist-Catholic amalgam." Afterward, Santeria remained largely underground in socialist Cuba and migrated to the United States with the exodus following Castro's rise to power.

In Cuba, as elsewhere in the New World, the Lukumi and other African religions evolved along several lines, depending on the predominant tribal makeup of the slave population. In French-controlled Haiti, Lukumi-Yoruba practices merged with those of Kongo-Anglo, the Fon, and Dahomeaneyan into a religion known as Voodoo (Vodun). Lukumi-Yoruba, Bantu, and Kongo people in Spanish and Portuguese colonies followed primarily Shango and Candomble in Brazil and Palo Monte and Lukumi-Yoruba in Cuba. Although the religious practices differ, there are similarities rooted in their common heritage. Shango and Eleggua, for instance, are worshipped in both Lukumi and Voodoo.

By the time the second major wave of slaves arrived in the eighteenth century, Cuba had a substantial middle class of Creoles — Andalusians, Galicians, and Basques, among a mosaic of other Spanish ethnicities. They were considered white. The African slaves and free blacks were called *negros de nación* (the Negro nations). They were grouped together according to their language and dialects, in much the same way that Apulians, Calabrians, and Sicilians all became Italians in the United States. In this way, the Lukumi — whether actually from Yorubaland or neighboring tribes or slaves sold by the Yoruba — came into bold relief. The word *Lukumi* was originally a greeting of a friend — someone from the same tribe or region or who spoke the same language or a close dialect.

The prominence of the Lukumi grew as their numbers increased, and for a time they outnumbered both Creoles and the nonwhite free population. Slaves in the Spanish empire could marry, own property, and even buy their freedom. By the eighteenth century, there was a higher proportion of free blacks in Cuba than in any other Caribbean island. Only after the end of the slave trade did the number of Europeans and Creoles again overtake the African population.

In Africa, the religious rites of the Lukumi were conducted openly by priests in temples — temples too small for large numbers of people but large enough for the sacred images of the *orishas* and to permit priests or priestesses to conduct rites. In Cuba, their religious practices were largely veiled from the public, except during high holidays.

In Cuba, the Lukumi religion became known as Santeria as a result of the practice of worshipping the *orishas* along with Catholic saints (*santos*). The *orishas* were venerated publicly according to Catholic rites and celebrations on the days of the various saints, as well as according to ancient Lukumi practices in private homes, clubs, and community associations. Those who were initiated became *santeros* or *santeras* (priests or priestesses). Hence, the Lukumi's religion became known as Santeria, or "the way of the saints."

In fact, the word *Santeria* originated as a pejorative term used by Catholic priests and the Spanish upper classes to describe the religious practices of Afro-Cuban slaves and peasants. Initially, it was applied indiscriminately to any Afro-Cuban priest, doctor, or sorcerer instead of only to those practicing the Lukumi religion and peasant or folk Catholicism. It was a derogatory reference to the unusual amount of devotion paid to the Catholic saints by Afro-Cuban worshippers, who had little regard for Jesus Christ or the teachings of scripture. In short, in pre-republic Cuba, Santeria was considered a pagan practice; only in the last fifty to sixty years was the word embraced by followers.

For a number of reasons, Santeria has been shrouded in secrecy, conducted under the guise of worshipping Catholic saints or in private homes. Because it is based on oral traditions, its rituals and symbolism become known only through initiation. High priests (*babalawos* and *iyaloshas*) are masters of divination and initiation rites. They train for years to learn the language, rites, and praises of the *orishas*, along with hundreds of prayers and songs.

The conditions of slavery, under the overarching supervision of the Catholic priests, did not permit the Lukumi to overtly pass down their traditions. Spanish law mandated that all slaves be baptized as Catholics when entering the West Indies, and they were to be buried according to Catholic rites in consecrated ground. The Cuban Fugitive Slave Law of 1789, for instance, stipulated that "All owners of slaves, of whatever class and condition that they are, must instruct them in the principles of the Catholic religion and in the true necessities in order that they be baptized within one year of their residence." In addition, the law dictated that slaves should not work on Catholic holidays, although in 1817, the diocesan bishop, under pressure from plantation owners, granted permission for them to work on Sundays.

As Georgetown University religious studies professor Joseph M. Murphy points out, conversion or adaptation to Catholicism, in contrast with Protestantism, may have facilitated the emergence of Santeria. Catholicism in Cuba gave greater stress to ceremonies — baptisms, saints' days, and funerals — than to knowledge of the scriptures. Catholic saints and ceremonies, unlike Protestant and Evangelical readings of the Bible, may therefore have been more easily accommodated by worshippers of the *orishas*. In Murphy's words:

> Catholicism offered a world of symbolism that could be translated into African meanings. The saints provided symbols behind which the *orisha* could live on. The more symbolically austere traditions of Protestantism did not have this panoply of sacred objects for Africans to identify and reinterpret. Catholic symbolism provided a haven for the *orishas*, symbolic building blocks to recreate the way of the *orishas* in the New World.

Moreover, Catholicism in colonial Cuba was a missionary movement aimed at converting slaves and indigenous peoples. Less important were ecclesiastical doctrines — the sacraments, extreme unction, the Eucharist, penitence, and holy orders. More important were Catholic images, miracle stories, and the yearly cycle of festivals for patron saints. There were also virtually insurmountable barriers to indoctrination into ecclesiastical doctrines. Language barriers, illiteracy, and enormous cultural and political differences set Catholic priests and colonial rulers apart from slaves, former slaves, and Amerindians.

There thus emerged a folk Catholicism in Cuba, as well as in Brazil, Mexico, and elsewhere. The differences between ecclesiastical and folk Catholicism are put well by Brandon:

> For the church, saints were human beings who led virtuous lives; they manifested in human form the spectacle of realized holiness. The folk, however, did not focus on the inner religiosity of the saints nor focus on them primarily as exemplary religious figures, models of what human beings should or could be. Instead they sought the external signs of the saints' ecclesiastical virtues, signs which could be manifested as forms of power and generosity that could make a difference in their own daily lives. For them the saints were human beings who had miraculous powers.

In other words, Cuban slaves were forced to convert to Catholicism and to observe its ceremonies, such as the christening of plantations and baptism for the newborn. Hence, they adapted, continuing to worship the *orishas* along with corresponding Catholic saints whose images they saw in churches and public squares and during ceremonies on holy days. In folk Catholicism, the miraculous images of saints became connected with specific festivals celebrating the awesome powers of patron saints and the *orishas*.

The Catholic liturgical calendar ordered life in Cuba, encouraging the adaptation of Lukumi practices of worship to Catholic celebrations. Shango became associated with St. Barbara's day, December 4, for instance. Oggun, the patron of war, became St. Peter. Oshun, the spirit of cooling river waters who controls money, love, and sensuality, became Our Lady of Charity. Ellegua, the *orisha* of the crossroads reigning over change and destiny, is identified with Anthony of Padua. Babalu Aye became St. Lazarus, the patron saint of the sick, celebrated on December 17. Table 1.1 illustrates the basic Santeria calendar of feasts, according to the day of the corresponding saint, the *orisha* worshipped, and the typical sacrifices made on each occasion.

Each *orisha* is associated with particular numbers, colors, foods, emblems, and dances. In particular, stones — stones thought to have come from Africa in the stomachs of slaves — are the embodiments of the *orishas*. They must be cared for lovingly, cleaned, and fed — sometimes with the blood of animals. These stones (*ota* in Yoruba and *otanes* in Spanish) embody the spiritual essence of the *orishas*. They are kept in clay tureens painted in the color of each *orisha*. They are fed with food offerings placed on top of the tureen; when animals are sacrificed, their blood is poured over them. Later, the stones and tureen are cleaned, the cover is replaced, and they are put in a safe place. They are not displayed publicly and are considered sacred. Only a few followers of Santeria have allowed them to be seen or photographed. Most followers consider that a sacrilege.

Ritual animal sacrifice is an integral part of the practices of the Lukumi and followers of Santeria. To remain strong and effective, the *orishas* (since they are alive) must eat. They require animal sacrifices and prepared dishes, along with human praises and prayers. Animals are sacrificed so that the *orishas* and humans may live. Their blood is offered to nourish the *orishas* and to bring good luck, clarity, and protection to worshippers. After most ceremonies, except for healing

Table 1.1 Santeria Calendar of Feasts

Date	Saint	*Orisha*	Function/Power	Sacrifice
Feb 2	Candelaria	Oya	Protection against death	Chickens, female goats, eggplants
June 6	Norbert	Ochosi	Hunting, jails	Roosters, pigeons
June 13	Anthony of Padua	Ellegua	Roads, gates, fate, justice, the unexpected	Candy, rum, cigars, chicken, fish
June 29	Peter	Oggun	Metals, weapons, sorcery, war, employment	Roosters, pigeons, blood, feathers
Sept 7	Regla	Yemaya	Protection of women, seas, fertility	Ducks, turtles, female goats, hens
Sept 8	Caridid	Oshun	Love, marriage, gold, money, sex	White hens, female goats, rum cake
Sept 24	Mercedes	Obatala	Peace, purity, wisdom, clarity	White doves, female goats
Oct 4	Francis	Ifa/Orumila	Divination, wisdom	Black hens, fruits, vegetables
Nov 16	Christopher	Aganyu	Control of enemies, fatherhood	Roosters, palm oil, crackers
Dec 4	Barbara	Shango	Power, passion, control of enemies	Lambs, goats, rats, red roosters, rams
Dec 17	Lazarus	Babalu Aye	Fires, illness, skin diseases	Cigars, pennies, water, pigeons

rites, the animals are cooked and eaten by the *santeros*. Thus, an old saying of *santeros* is *La sangre para el Santo, la carne para el santero* ("Blood for the saint, meat for the *santero*").

———

In Cuba, the emergence of Santeria was reinforced by Afro-Cubans mixing together and preserving remnants of their religion in Havana social clubs or mutual aid societies, known as *cabildos*. In the mid-eighteenth century, Havana's Bishop Pedro Augustin Morel de Santa Cruz campaigned to bring Catholicism to the Afro-Cuban clubs and to establish a formal *cabildo* system, as in Spain. In Spain, *cabildos* were religious brotherhoods functioning as social clubs and mutual aid societies. Their main activities involved initiating new members into Catholicism, venerating the saints, and participating in festivals on holy days, notably, by bearing the images of saints in parades and carnivals.

In Spain, the *cabildos* were organized around particular trades and occupations. In Cuba, they were organized along the ethnic lines of the organizations of *negros de nación* and Afro-Cuban social clubs. They nonetheless served the same religious, social, mutual aid, and public celebratory functions. Each was made up of Afro-Cubans of the same *nación* and was allowed to continue some traditions, such as dancing, drum beating, and religious devotion, as long as they were organized around Catholic festivals.

It was in the *cabildos* that the language of the Lukumi became the ritual language of Santeria. The importance of the *cabildos* in promoting the merger of Lukumi *orishas* and Catholic saints is underscored by the fact that, unlike in urban Cuba, in rural areas there were no schools or formal associations, and frequently no churches either. The Catholic priests' promotion of *cabildos* thus preserved the Lukumi religion in Havana and a few other cities. By 1839, the Lukumi had established themselves, or rather reestablished an older Afro-Cuban club, as the Cabildo Africano Lukumi under patron saint Barbara. On St. Barbara's festival day, the Lukumi would dance in the streets of Havana under the saint's image, in scarlet and white, to the beating of *bata* drums and rhythms passed down according to oral tradition.

In the Havana *cabildos*, the religious practices of the Lukumi were transformed into what became known as Santeria. As Brandon explains:

The urban *cabildo* . . . provided the place for the reconstruction of the African priesthood and for communal worship. Here drumming, song, and dance came together in the drama of the *orisha* made visible in the bodies of the devotees. . . . Inside the *cabildo*, ancestor veneration came to refer to the lines of ancestral priests and priestesses and blood kinship became ritual kinship after the manner of the Catholic institution of *compadrazgo*. The sons and daughters of the *orisha* became the *ajihados* and *ajihadas* (godchildren) of the priests. All the godchildren constituted a religious family of brothers and sisters. There was a fusion of the Nigerian and Catholic institutions such that it is not possible to separate them and tell where one starts and the other stops.

In sum, a religious structure integrating the *orishas* and Catholic saints emerged. Whereas in Yorubaland the *orishas* were worshipped by separate families, lineages, and priests, by the late eighteenth century in Cuba, all priests and *cabildos* came together under a large religious umbrella. The *cabildos* exercised the only collective authority over followers of Santeria. In their meetings, the *babalawos* maintained the laws and practices governing their religion. Otherwise, unlike the Catholic hierarchy, the *santeros* worked their spirits and magic independently and secretly, according to their initiations.

Over a couple of centuries, Santeria, which appeared to be a folk version of Catholicism, spread to white indentured plantation workers, slave owners, and other middle-class urban residents. Initially, membership had extended to only Lukumi and later to non-Yoruba Afro-Cubans. After the end of slave trading, membership became open to all through initiation rites. Others were brought into the religion as a result of interracial marriages, contact between poor white peasants working in the fields alongside former slaves, and upper-class Creoles and whites who had been initiated by household servants or sought counsel from Lukumi diviners.

In these various ways, the *orishas* became the defining feature of Santeria, regardless of worshippers' physical appearance or actual ethnic or racial heritage. Although the religion was rooted in the ancient traditions of ancestor worship of the slaves from Yorubaland, the Lukumi-Santeria worshippers became multicultural and multiracial, and the rites were open to all who had been initiated into the secrets of the *orishas*.

Ironically, although the Catholic Church had initially promoted the *cabildos*, increasingly restrictive laws gradually curbed them. Over time, this led to the disintegration of the *cabildos* and drove *santeros* further underground by the end of the nineteenth century. The 1792 Good Government Law, for instance, forbade *cabildos* to stage traditional dances and *bata* drum beating on any day except for Sunday or festival days for the saints. Other processions were restricted to the hours before and after Catholic masses. Subsequent laws in the 1830s and 1840s barred all dancing sponsored by the *cabildos* and the holding of burial rites "in the manner of their land" — that is, according to traditional African religious practices. Not surprisingly, Lukumi religious practices were further submerged in Catholic festivals or conducted privately in homes.

During Cuba's wars for independence — the Ten Years War from 1868 to 1878, during which the Catholic Church's influence began to wane, and the War for Independence from 1895 to 1898, which ended with the Treaty of Paris giving control of Cuba to the United States — the *cabildos* were reformulated as semiunderground cults. Each took on a slightly different identity according to its lineage and operated largely autonomously. The black Cuban population subsequently became more organized and mobilized, culminating in an ill-fated uprising in 1912 that resulted in the massacre of several thousand black men. The uprising nonetheless helped lay to rest the colonial plantation class's economic dominance and contributed to the growing influence of the Creole middle class, even though it reinforced underlying racial prejudices.

In the first decades of the twentieth century, the struggles among competing groups and classes continued. Violence, assassinations, and repression, along with gangsterism and political corruption, were prevelant. The *cabildos* were finally forbidden to operate as affiliations of the Catholic Church. Some remained active as mutual aid societies, though under an even greater veil of secrecy. The Cabildo Africano Lukumi was reorganized as a mutual aid society in 1891 and was later reorganized again in light of the changing political and legal currents. Divorced from any official connection with the Catholic Church, the Lukumi *cabildo* nonetheless continued to hold processions and masses on St. Barbara's day.

Cuba gained independence on May 20, 1902, and in the decades that followed, the proportion of Cubans who had been born in Africa decreased. Followers of Santeria became more multicultural and even more secretive in the face of a wave of nationalism that swept the new republic. The new nationalism resulted in a campaign of Europeanization that denigrated the African heritage of the island. The Ku Klux Klan Kubano and other anti-black groups came into prominence in

Cuba. The campaign to de-Africanize Cuba led, once again, to the persecution of *santeros*, the confiscation of religious paraphernalia, and the enactment of laws forbidding the use of ritual *bata* drums. Santeria was pushed further underground.

Santeria evolved into secret societies, or extended families, organized around senior priests or priestesses, with only a thin or no veneer of Catholicism. Each high priest or priestess presides as the head of a house (*ile*, or *casa* in Spanish) or, in a deeper sense, a family. They preside over initiation rites and ceremonies of rebirth and become the godfathers or godmothers of extended families "in the spirit" *(en santo)*. The secrecy of initiation rites and the lack of public temples mean that the rituals are usually performed at the private residences of *santeros*. At critical times, most Cubans seek consultations with such high priests or priestesses, and virtually all followers are former clients who had sought advice or healing. Through initiation rites, they become part of the family of the high priest or priestess, assume responsibilities of devotion, and make a lifelong commitment to a particular *orisha*.

In the 1940s, when there was greater religious freedom for Protestants and others in Cuba, Lukumi-Santeria was still not recognized as an official religion. It remained submerged, at best considered part of the Afro-Cuban folk heritage, or dismissed disparagingly as witchcraft practiced by uneducated, lower-class blacks. Early writers on the religion, such as Dr. Don Fernando Ortiz and later Lydia Cabrera, thus portrayed Lukumi-Santeria as fetishism and folklore, further reinforcing the perceived need among *santeros* for secrecy.

In the early part of the twentieth century, another influence on many followers of Santeria came into play, namely, Espiritismo. Espiritismo, a variant of spiritualism, was founded in France by Hippolyte Rivail, who wrote under the pseudonym Allan Kardec. Espiritismo combined scientism with Christian moral teachings and personal mysticism, although it ran counter to Catholicism in maintaining that clairvoyants could communicate directly with saints and the spirits of the dead.

Espiritismo appealed to middle- and upper-class urbanites in Cuba, Puerto Rico, and elsewhere. It had a special attraction for those who were antagonistic toward the Catholic hierarchy; those interested in science, spiritualism, and progressive ideas; and *independistas,* or spiritualists practicing more than one faith, such as Carmen Pla. The popularity of Espiritismo was understandable, given the wave of Europeanism that swept Cuba after the founding of the republic.

Followers of Espiritismo gathered in private homes and sat around tables draped with white cloths. On the tables might be placed candles, a vase of flowers, a cigar, and an image of a spirit, ancestor, or deceased loved one. Then they would invoke the saints and spirits in a séance, falling into trances and communicating with them.

Espiritismo was "chameleon like," in that it absorbed elements of both folk Catholicism and Santeria. As Brandon observes:

> In Cuba Kardec's spirit guides frequently embodied the popular stereotypic images of Cuban ethnic, racial, and professional groups. Not only did Cuban espiritistas in their mediumistic trance manifest spirit guides that resembled themselves, both physically and in temperament, but both black and white mediums manifested spirit guides who were *Africanos de nacions*—Lukumi, Mandinga, Mina, and Congolese tribesmen who had suffered and died in slavery. None of this was in Kardec.

Moreover, Espiritismo was both different from and similar to Santeria. As Brandon further explains:

> Espiritistas made fine distinctions within the world of the dead which Santeria did not make and generalized those which it did. . . . Even though Espiritismo had saints, they were different. In Espiritismo the saints were pure and remote and not at the ready call of the medium; instead, mediums relied on a variety of lesser and more accessible spirits. As a result the spirit guides and angel guardians of Espiritismo were lumped together with the saints or *orisha;* in turn the saints or *orisha* assumed new roles as protectors, spirit guides, and guardian angels.

Large numbers of white middle- and upper-class Cubans, though nominally Catholic, were attracted to Espiritismo and Santeria. Like Carmen Pla and her sons, many fled in the aftermath of Castro's rise to power. By this time, the blending of Catholicism, Espiritismo, and Lukumi-Santeria was evident in the fact that *babalawos* and *espiritistas* usually required Catholic baptism for initiates prior to their induction into Santeria.

————

On the eve of the Cuban revolution, there was a rich kaleidoscope of religious practices, overlaid and interwoven with Afro-Cuban religions, folk Catholicism, and Espiritismo. For most Cubans, however, the lines were clear, even as different religious traditions mixed, depending on the individual *babalawos* and *iyaloshas*. Catholic priests and some of their parishioners looked down on folk Catholicism and Santeria, but many Catholics consulted *santeros* on occasion. Some *santeros* venerated primarily Catholic saints but made offerings of herbs, tobacco, and fruit in the Lukumi tradition at altars for the saints. Some knew traditional Lukumi verses and prayers, but others knew very little or none of the language. Other followers did not keep altars of saints in their homes but instead had only the stones and statues of the *orishas* and made offerings in Lukumi rites, even though they associated the *orishas* with the days and powers of Catholic saints. Still others strictly observed the traditions of Lukumi and paid no attention to Catholic saints. Finally, some *santeros* were less scrupulous in offering their services. They were, frankly, more concerned about making money.

After Castro's rise to power, the status of Santeria remained no less ambiguous. *Santeros* fought on both sides of the war against Fulgencio Batista. Certainly, *santeros* continued to follow somewhat different practices, ranging from those (probably the majority) who worshipped the *orishas* along with the saints to those who completely rejected Catholic symbols and statues. And although many *santeros* fled Cuba, many more stayed, particularly poor black followers.

The Catholic Church, including the Vatican, initially supported Castro's overthrow of Batista's government. Only afterward did the Vatican and the Cuban Catholic hierarchy become concerned about religious freedom. When priests became involved in protests, they were accused of counterrevolutionary acts. After the aborted Bay of Pigs invasion, it was reported that two priests had participated. As a result, priests were arrested, and Catholic churches were closed. Subsequently, parochial schools were eliminated when education was nationalized, and church property was confiscated.

Followers of Santeria never faced the kind of repression that Catholics confronted. Even Catholic churches were permitted to reopen in 1965–1966, as long as they did not proselytize. In short, repression alternated with tolerance. Although Santeria was never officially recognized, it remained widely practiced. As Pablo Linares, a Havana *babalawo* and fifth-generation Santeria priest, put it: "We never experienced persecution; we just had to be discreet."

Castro's government, unlike some other communist regimes, claimed that there was no contradiction between religion and socialism. It could hardly have been otherwise. Castro's revolution depended on the support of poor black Cubans, particularly in rural areas, where most of the population identified with Santeria. *Santeros,* having fought in the revolution, held positions in the military and the government under Castro. Even high-ranking government officials both before and after the revolution were believed to practice Santeria. Gerardo Machado, president of Cuba from 1925 to 1933, was considered a son of Shango. Carlos Prio Socarras, president from 1948 to 1952, was a known devotee of Ifa and had a *babalawo* as a well-known adviser. Likewise, Fulgencio Batista, president from 1940 to 1944 and again from 1952 to 1959, was widely reputed to be a *santero.*

At times, Castro embraced the symbolism of Santeria as well. In January 1959, during his first televised speech, a white dove landed on his shoulder and another perched on the podium. Both stayed throughout his two-hour oration. The international press reported the "freakish" appearance of the "doves of peace," but for many Catholics, the white doves represented the Holy Spirit, and for followers of Santeria, they symbolized the divinity of Obatala — the *orisha* who molds humans of clay. For both, the doves were a sign of supernatural powers. Castro was a messiah.

Pichardo does not believe that Castro is a *santero.* But at least one scholar who studied Castro's use of Santeria symbols, Ivor L. Miller, concludes that the "transculturation" — a term first used by Don Fernando Ortiz — is unmistakable: from the white doves to stories of Castro's initiation into Santeria and his use of red and black (the colors of Ellegua) in Cuba's flag. "On the one hand," Miller observes, "symbolic dates, doves, acronyms, and colors have been used by Castro to motivate Cuba's population. On the other, Santeria practitioners actively read his actions and character in ways that associate Castro with Lukumi divinities. This type of dialogic is inescapable in the Caribbean, and is one reason politicians are able to use symbols to their advantage." Notably, though, he concludes:

> Whether or not Castro is an initiate is irrelevant. The fact that many Cubans feel Castro is a *santero* underscores the popular belief that in a world filled with enemies, only someone with extraordinary power can be protected (as Castro has been) for over 30 years. Since Cuban mythology teaches that supranatural powers are accessed through working with the Santeria divinities, and Castro has publicly demonstrated his use of their symbols, he must therefore be working with them.

In fact, Castro's government embraced Afro-Cuban dances and songs as expressions of the cultural, artistic, and folk heritage of "the new Cuban state." In the 1970s, when Cuba was sending troops to African countries to fight in their wars of independence, the government recruited *santeros* to promote Santeria as the national folklore in the *Conjunto Folklorico Nacional de Cuba*. But this outreach proved coercive as well. If *santeros* refused to participate in the *Conjunto Folklorico*, they were arrested for offering their services without a work permit and sentenced to hard labor on remote farms. Only by participating could they remain in Havana. Yet if they independently registered as priests or priestesses, they were barred from working in the government. Therefore, those who worked in the government did not publicly acknowledge practicing Santeria.

Santeria remained shrouded in secrecy. Some *santeros* and other spiritualists, of course, could not square the government's recognition of Afro-Cuban religions as part of the country's folk heritage with its socialist policies or, for that matter, with Santeria's tradition of secrecy. Others feared that openness would bring more repression. Castro's government did arrest members of Afro-Cuban religions on the pretext that they held ceremonies on days other than those designated by the government, but whether they were also opponents of Castro remains disputed. Beyond dispute is that the government's rationing of food and the ending of private enterprises contributed to the secrecy of the *santeros* and to their development of an underground economy for trading animals and other items used in religious ceremonies.

———

Santeria Comes to America

Ernesto Pichardo arrived in South Florida with the first major wave of Cuban exiles. Over the next couple of decades, these immigrants changed the complexion and politics of that region. Cubans had earlier come to Florida, New York, and Texas; and in the late 1880s, Cuban communities had been established in other parts of Florida. In Tampa, for instance, a large Cuban population had been established in Yorba City. Still, there is no evidence that the *orishas* were worshipped there. Although there were a few known practicing *santeros* in the United States in the 1940s and 1950s, it was not until the 1960s that substantial numbers of followers of Santeria arrived.

By the 1980s, there were an estimated 50,000 to 100,000 followers of Santeria in South Florida. More than 90 percent of them were Cuban Americans. That number grew substantially as a result of the 1980 Mariel boatlift following Castro's deportation of some 125,000 Cubans, many of whom had been imprisoned. It is estimated that a large percentage were followers of Santeria or became so after arriving in the United States. Like their enslaved Yoruba ancestors in Cuba centuries ago, they found themselves in a strange and inhospitable culture, in yet another diaspora. Disoriented and uncertain, they sought guidance from the *orishas*.

As Teresita Pedraza, a Cuban-born sociologist at Miami-Dade Community College, stresses: "You have to place yourself into the daily life of those practicing the religion. Perceive a world that has been largely hostile to them. Even Cubans who have been financially successful have suffered through a severe social dislocation. Although Cuba has never been more than nominally Catholic, many Cubans turned to the church after the revolution, praying for a miracle. The miracle never happened. So they turned to other, perhaps more powerful, solutions."

The complexion of Miami changed dramatically in other ways after the first wave of Cuban immigrants. In the 1960s, about 75 percent of Miami was Anglo — Jewish, Greek, Italian, and so forth. By the 1980s, Anglos constituted only 15 percent of the population. The other 85 percent included Cubans, Haitians, Salvadorans, Jamaicans, Puerto Ricans, Nicaraguans, and others.

Moreover, whereas the Cubans who arrived in the first wave of immigrants in the early 1960s were known as the "Promising Ones," those who came in the 1980 Mariel boatlift became known as the "Frightening Ones." Whereas the first brought predominantly white, middle- to upper-class professionals, the second brought a greater number of black Cubans from the lower socioeconomic strata of society. Following the Mariel boatlift, drug dealing and killings skyrocketed by almost 20 percent in Miami-Dade County.

When the controversy erupted over Pichardo's opening of the Church of the Lukumi Babalu Aye in 1987, Santeria remained a minority religion in South Florida. A study of the religious demographics of Broward, Miami-Dade, and Palm Beach Counties found that Catholics and Jews predominated. There were 141 Roman Catholic churches with 703,249 parishioners and 136 synagogues with 489,800 members. Southern Baptists were next in number, with 172 churches and 142,974 members, followed by United Methodists with 107 churches and a congregation of 66,458, Episcopalians with 69 established churches and 37,247 adherents, and Presbyterians with 56 churches and 22,398 members. Admittedly, the reported numbers may have failed to account for those who did not actively belong to a church or who claimed to be Catholic, for example, but actually practiced more than one religion. Nevertheless, the figures highlight the religious diversity in South Florida.

Santeria's practice of animal sacrifice was receiving considerable public attention, not only in Miami but around the country. Almost daily, animal carcasses were found on the front steps of Miami's courthouses and jails, offerings for the protection of those who were arrested, on trial, or in jail. In New York City, there was outrage over reports of a goat's head and paper bags filled with chicken feet and blood-smeared paper dolls being found in Central Park. In Atlantic City and elsewhere, people were arrested for cruelty to animals when police found animal carcasses at ritual sites. In Falls Church, Virginia, a cemetery was reportedly the site of animal sacrifice, with police repeatedly finding gutted chickens and the remains of other animals.

And in Santa Monica, California, the sacrifice of three lambs and a dozen chickens reportedly caused an overflow of blood from a basement drain into an apartment complex parking lot.

Santeria was also portrayed in then-popular television shows such as *Miami Vice*, in which actors Don Johnson and Philip Michael Thomas played Sonny Crockett and Richardo Tubbs, modeled after two real-life Miami-Dade detectives. For a while, Pichardo served as a technical adviser for the show.

Even more dramatic was the discovery in early 1989 of the bodies of over a dozen murdered men in Matamoros, Mexico. In a kind of feeding frenzy, the media blamed the killings on Santerians. A police investigation eventually concluded that the murders had been orchestrated by a gang of drug runners who were seeking protection from the police. As it happened, members of the gang did practice ritual sacrifice, and the leader of the gang had required members to watch some fourteen times the movie *The Believers*, in which elements of Santeria were combined with human sacrifice.

In the District of Columbia, New York City, and elsewhere, local officials forced some *santeros* to sign agreements not to sacrifice animals during ceremonies, as a result of pressure brought by animal rights advocates and health and safety inspectors. News reports in the *Miami Herald, Washington Post, New York Times,* and *Los Angeles Times* led to the controversy over the Church of the Lukumi becoming known as "the chicken wars."

———

Such was the tumultuous history of how the Lukumi religion became known as Santeria in Cuba and later in the United States. By the time Pichardo and his family were preparing to open the Church of the Lukumi Babalu Aye in Hialeah, Cubans had transformed South Florida, and Santeria was entering the popular culture. Santeria was identified with animal sacrifices and was associated with drug dealing, crime, and poorly educated immigrants. Mainstream religious leaders, health and law enforcement officials, and animal rights advocates generally looked down on, if not vehemently opposed, Santeria.

Ernesto Pichardo and his family were true believers. In founding the first Church of the Lukumi, they aimed to preserve the memories, traditions, and powers of the *orishas.* They sought to institutionalize the religion as it had been passed down from their spiritual ancestors. They had nothing to do with the Catholic saints of most Cuban *santeros*. The opening of the Church of the Lukumi thus broke with the traditional understanding of most *santeros* and Cubans in South Florida, as well as sparked fierce opposition from animal rights supporters and others.

CHAPTER 2

The Chicken Wars

In Little Havana, Ernesto Pichardo was initiated into the worship of the *orishas* at the age of sixteen. Like other young initiates, he had suffered a "serious illness" and was destined to become a priest. Most followers of Santeria begin as clients of a *santero* and are initiated later, in middle age. Pichardo entered the priesthood in the order of Shango, ordained by Oni Shango Agba Lagba Juvenal Ortega Shango Dina. His brother was also initiated and became a *babalawo*.

Four years later, in 1974, the Church of the Lukumi Babalu Aye was founded by Ernesto and Fernando Pichardo; their mother, *iyalosha* Carmen Pla Oni Yemaya; *babalosha* Raul Rodriguez, their stepfather; and attorney Gino Negretti. The church was incorporated as a nonprofit organization under its founder, Carmen Pla (Rodriguez), and according to the spiritual mandates of Encarnación de la Caridad y Rodriguez, an Oshun spirit. Fernando Pichardo became its corporate secretary and chief administrator, and Ernesto Pichardo was named corporate president and point person for public relations. The roles of the two brothers were fitting. Fernando is reserved, whereas Ernesto is provocative, outspoken, and at times brash.

Their spiritual elders in Cuba had tried unsuccessfully to establish a church back in the 1940s. In retrospect, establishing the Church of the Lukumi was a no less daunting challenge, though in different ways. The eventual lawsuit and its outcome, Pichardo says, "sealed what had been tried before." The result was official public recognition of the Lukumi traditions as a religion, not merely as a cultural artifact or part of Afro-Cuban folklore.

In 1978, Pichardo helped organize a three-day conference of religious scholars, Catholics, and *santeros* at the University of Miami under the sponsorship of the Florida Endowment for the Humanities. The church also held an ordination rite for its patron *orisha*

Babalu Aye at the Oyotunji ("Oyo again wakes") African Village in Sheldon, South Carolina, about a half mile off U.S. Route 17, which runs from Savannah, Georgia, to Charleston.

Holding the ceremony at the Oyotunji Village remains revealing. The Oyotunji Village was founded in 1970 by *oba* Ofuntola Osejiman Adelabu Adefunmi I. Adefunmi, born Walter King in Detroit in 1928, had been baptized at age twelve in the Baptist Church. He later withdrew from that church to study African religions and eventually moved to New York. In 1954, he joined the African nationalist movement and worked with Haitian Voodoo practitioners, as well as aligned himself with the remaining members of Marcus Garvey's old Africanist movement in Harlem. In 1959, shortly before the Cuban revolution, he went to Matanzas, Cuba, and was initiated into Santeria as an *obatala* priest, the first African American to do so. Upon returning to the United States, he founded the Shango Temple, which was later incorporated as the African Theological Archministry, moved to East Harlem, and subsequently renamed the Yoruba Temple. In the turbulent 1960s, when black nationalism was on the rise, Adefunmi celebrated African religion and culture. He taught that the core of Santeria, Voodoo, and Candomble was *orisha*-Voodoo worship.

Adefunmi initially relied on Cuban and Puerto Rican *santeros* to help legitimate the Yoruba Temple, but their relationship became increasingly strained. His teaching of black nationalism turned off many white *santeros* (and virtually all the Cuban *santeros* in the United States at the time were white), and they resented his dismissal of the Catholic saints. Moreover, his public temple outraged those who adhered to the tradition of secrecy and viewed it as integral to Santeria. In 1965, members of his Yoruba Temple performed at the African Pavilion at the World's Fair in New York. Although such performances attracted new members, Cuban *santeros* grew angrier about his violation of the secrecy taboo and his elimination of all representations of the saints. In short, Cuban *santeros* living in the United States could not understand Santeria without the *santos* and recoiled at Adefunmi's black nationalism.

After a series of confrontations and death threats, Adefunmi closed the Yoruba Temple, left New York, and founded the Oyotunji Village. There, he re-created a traditional Yoruba village, complete with temples and shrines for the *orishas*. It was open to the public, and he initiated priests into the religion without the advice of any Cuban *santeros*. He gave African names to his followers and encouraged them to use them publicly, as well as to dress in the traditional Lukumi attire of colorful flowing robes.

The Church of the Lukumi's ordination ceremony at the Oyotunji Village signified their common ground but highlighted their differences as well. Both Adefunmi and the church's founders sought to purify or reform the religion known as Santeria. Yet the ceremony performed by white Cuban immigrants was held at a place that did not honor the *santos* of Santeria and instead glorified the African origins of the religion. That struck some *santeros* as illegitimate, and it invoked racist and derogatory associations with uneducated, lower-class black practitioners in Cuba. Unquestionably, the Church of the Lukumi was on a collision course with the larger Cuban community, including many followers of Santeria.

Although Adefunmi and the Church of the Lukumi shared common ground in reclaiming the purity of the *orishas*, each sought a reformation leading in a very different direction. Adefunmi focused on the African roots of the religion to promote black pride and self-determination, whereas for Pichardo and the Church of the Lukumi, the *orishas* represented universal truths open to all initiates. In other words, both were on the fringes of Santeria, minorities within a religious minority.

In coming together, each sought legitimacy for their organization. In addition, as Pichardo explained, divinations had told them that they would be asked to perform the ceremony at the Oyotunji Village, so they never questioned doing so, in spite of Adefunmi's black nationalism. As it turned out, Adefunmi had been initiated in Cuba by the Pichardos' spiritual godfather. They thus shared the same lineage and common ancestors.

————

A decade after its founding, the Church of the Lukumi still had no physical presence, no building in which to conduct its ceremonies, and it would not have one for nearly another decade. It remained a dream of the founders, who continued conducting initiations, providing counseling, and organizing *santeros* in South Florida.

Pichardo and the church were caught off guard by the increased demands brought by the influx of Cubans from the Mariel boatlift. The church, he recalls, was as overwhelmed as Miami-Dade County's departments of health, safety, and law enforcement. Consequently, in 1983, the church established the Institute for New World Studies, funded by the Florida Endowment for the Humanities. It conducted workshops on Afro-Caribbean religions for law enforcement officials, hospital and mental health professionals, academics, and the general public.

Ernesto Pichardo also took the lead in trying to resolve the growing number of disputes between *santeros* and city officials. In 1984, for instance, he persuaded the Dade County School Board to allow a third-grade student to miss school for a month in order to be initiated into the religion. As Frank Howard, an attorney for the school board, explained: "In this instance, the compulsory attendance laws must give way to the freedom of religion laws. We have concluded that the absence of up to a month is a religious necessity when a person is being initiated into the priesthood of Santeria." As Pichardo observed at the time, "Just as Christians and Jews are allowed their activities, this is a gain [for followers of Santeria] in that respect." Over the years and with each conflict, he grew more tenacious and defensive of religious freedom.

The following year, the church intervened in disputes between thirteen *santeros* and humane society officials who charged them with violating laws against animal cruelty. Under the church's auspices, the first courses on Afro-Caribbean religions were offered through Miami-Dade Community College. Pichardo also coauthored a book (in Spanish), *Oduduwa Obatala*, on the religion and served as a consultant for the Tri-Star film *The Band on the Hand.*

By 1986, the Church of the Lukumi, in conjunction with the Mental Health Association of Dade County, was offering accredited courses on Afro-Caribbean religions to local law enforcement officers. By this time, the church had an ongoing campaign to recruit new members and officers from among senior *santeros* in Miami-Dade County. It had formed a sixteen-member committee to organize for the formal opening of the Church of the Lukumi Babalu Aye in Hialeah.

The Purity of Spirit

In preparing for the public opening of the Church of the Lukumi Babalu Aye, Ernesto and Fernando Pichardo, their mother, and a few others aimed to institutionalize the religion and preserve the purity of the Lukumi faith. In a statement of purpose for the church, Ernesto Pichardo made their objectives clear:

- To maintain, own, operate, and have a secured religious place of worship, according to the teachings of the Lukumi/Ayoba religion.
- To hold sessions and ceremonies for the worship of ancestors.
- To perform traditional baptism, marriage, birth rite, priesthood ordination, and death rite.
- To engage in the certification of its ordained members.
- To take appropriate legal action to ensure our constitutional protection of religious freedom.

Institutionalization of the religion under the auspices of the Church of the Lukumi alarmed both those opposed to the religion and many within the Santeria community. The concerns, even outrage, of outsiders — Catholics, Protestants of various denominations, and animal rights activists — are in some ways easier to understand than those of other *santeros*. In aiming to institutionalize and open to the public the Church of the Lukumi, Pichardo and his family sought a reformation — a purification and unification of priests and practices according to their understanding of the worship of the *orishas*. As Pichardo declared: "Institutionalization in ways of formal tribal order should serve as pillars to unite our communities worldwide. The focal point must be the collective welfare of the religion, its institutions, and not personal human grandeur. The *orishas* are the leaders and the ministers their servants."

In many ways, their plans were threatening to the *santeros*, particularly those devoted to Catholic saints. First, the Church of the Lukumi appeared to impose a hierarchy and a litany impinging on the freedom of particular lineages of individual *santeros*. Traditionally, there were no leaders, no hierarchy, and no written doctrine. *Babalawos* and *iyaloshas* were simply high priests and priestesses, "the mouthpieces of the *orishas*," who offered guidance and instruction on the mysteries of life. Even in the old *cabildo* system in Cuba, the independence of the *santeros* had been largely respected, except during the periodic meetings held to reach agreement on rules governing their practices or to divine a forecast for the coming year.

Although the Lukumi-Santeria religion was based on oral traditions, Pichardo promulgated a Declaration on the Life of Priests that appeared to show contempt for the individualism and idiosyncratic ways of many *santeros*. In Pichardo's view, though, many young followers of Santeria wanted a "religious experience in premature ways," while some older *santeros* were "deficient in universal teachings." What was needed was a return to the "long-term traditional apprenticeship" of those initiated into the religion. It was precisely this "lack of religious education" that was at the root of the problems confronting those both inside and outside the religion in South Florida in the 1980s. The universal teachings were too often neglected or sacrificed by the idiosyncratic practices of many *santeros*, particularly by the recent arrivals from the Mariel boatlift.

The priesthood, according to Pichardo, had "to unite and function in one body of common purpose." It had to move beyond "clan or informal tribal systems," beyond the particular lineages of individual *babalawos* and *iyaloshas*, in order to become a "world religion." "Those ordained are ministers of *orishas*," Pichardo stated in his Declaration on the Life of Priests:

> As ministers they are a living symbol of sacrifice. They perform the sacred duty of sacrifice so that the offerings can be made acceptable and blessed by the *orishas* in the name of *Olodumare* [heavenly father]. The spiritual sacrifice is offered in union with the *orishas* in ways pleasing to *Olodumare*. Therefore each ordained person has a responsibility in his or her individualism and in relation to the human family.
>
> Priests and priestesses are bound together by the sacred word and teachings of the *orishas* not by their individualistic criteria. As educators of the faith, by themselves or through others, they must teach the faithful and lead them into a mature relationship with the *orishas* as the central point.

Such doctrines went against the understanding of many followers of Santeria. In the United States, as in Cuba, most *santeros* operated out of their homes or in the back rooms of *botanicas*. Like being a Catholic priest, being a *babalawo* or an *iyalosha* was deemed a full-time job, except that they worked independently within their extended families and communities.

First, establishing a formal hierarchy appeared to be a crass power grab and was financially threatening. Many *santeros* balked at paying a $250 fee for certification in addition to paying annual dues to the Church of the Lukumi. Moreover, each ceremony and rite had a price. An initiation rite, for example, could cost $10,000, more or less, depending on the number of *orishas* involved. Since the initiates become the godchildren of a *babalawo* or *iyalosha* — part of a large, extended family — they continue to offer gifts and donations in exchange for services. As Teresita Pedraza emphasizes, *santeros* provide a service for displaced people: "The key element is that a *santero* listens to you. Your problem becomes his problem. You immediately acquire an extended family, a network of support. In the home of *santeros*, there is always food, and he may be able to help you find a job, or get off drugs. It becomes a personal challenge for the *santero* to help you." Given such personal and spiritual connections, most *santeros* saw little need to submit to a new, overarching, hierarchical institutional structure.

Second, just as *santeros* more than a decade earlier had challenged Adefunmi's Yoruba Temple for breaking the tradition of secrecy, many *santeros* in South Florida objected to establishing the Church of the Lukumi and to publicly displaying ancient, secret rites, especially ritual animal sacrifice. Admittedly, by the mid-1980s, an increasing number of books explaining Santeria had appeared, but some *santeros* still considered going public offensive, a sacrilege. Others worried that the publicity would only invite more hostility from humane societies and law enforcement officials, leading to more confrontations and arrests on charges of animal cruelty.

Third, sparking opposition from *santeros* was the Church of the Lukumi's rejection of the saints and the matter of syncretism — the traditional merging of the *orishas* and Catholic saints. Many *santeros* saw no difference between the *orishas* and the saints. As Donald Cosentino, a lecturer on African religions at the University of California–Los Angeles, explained with respect to the practice of animal sacrifice: "It's very similar to a Catholic Mass. There is a transfer of body and blood, which you offer up to the Father, and then consume it yourself. Catholicism holds that the Crucifixion was the ultimate sacrifice, and no other could measure up. Santeria is more like the Old Testament, in that they continue to make blood sacrifices."

The matter of whether the religion is syncretic remains complex and controversial. In light of its history in Cuba, Santeria is usually portrayed as the syncretism of the Lukumi and Catholic religions. As Migene Gonzales-Wippler, a Puerto Rican author of several books on Santeria, observed: "Santeria is a typical case of syncretism, the spontaneous, popular combination or reconciliation of different religious beliefs. This syncretism can be appreciated in the fact that all of the Yoruba deities worshiped in Santeria have been identified with Catholic saints." And she emphasized: "The Yoruba did not simply accept Catholic saints — they *identified* them with the *orishas*. Santeria means literally 'the worship of the saints,' and these saints are identified with the *orishas* of the Yoruba pantheon. This is a typical case of syncretism."

Hence arose a syncretic tradition — bilingual, bicultural, and bi-religious — in which Lukumi *orishas* and Catholic saints are invoked as manifestations of the same divine spirits. In the words of Joseph M. Murphy: "As the Yoruba had become Lukumi in Cuba, so the Yoruba religious vision had become Santeria, an attempt to honor the gods of Africa in the land of Catholic saints."

However, most followers of Santeria recognize differences between the *orishas* and the saints, or at least treat them differently. For instance, the sacred *orisha* stones are concealed in clay pots kept in cabinets, away from public view, whereas *santeros* who pray to Catholic saints keep their statues on top of cabinets, on altars, or on shelves, in plain view. Moreover, only the *orisha* stones are nourished in sacrificial rites. The saints are never fed the blood of sacrificed animals. In some homes, African images and symbols are worshipped solely according to Lukumi traditions, while Catholic saints are worshipped in the manner of folk Catholicism and in Spanish. Thus, old *santeros* in Cuba reportedly spoke of Catholicism as *el camino de los blancos* ("the way, or path, of the whites") and of Santeria as *el camino de los negros* ("the way, or path, of the blacks").

Santeria's so-called syncretism remains problematic in other ways. It oversimplifies the multiple transformations that took place in Cuba. Santeria, as even Gonzales-Wippler admitted, "is a religion entirely

{ *Animal Sacrifice and Religious Freedom* }

independent from that of the Yoruba, even though its general structure is largely based on the Yoruba tradition."

Although Ernesto Pichardo and the other founders of the Church of the Lukumi embraced the word *Santeria*, they gradually became convinced that it was a misnomer and in some ways misleading. For them, the religion was emphatically not syncretic. The *santos* were distracting baggage picked up during the centuries of covert religious practice in Cuba.

"There has been a cultural syncreticism," Pichardo explained, "but applying it to the religion it does not hold. A number of people are syncretic, at a low level of religious transition. If we truly look at the religion, it is not syncretic. There is nothing we do that draws on or feeds on another religion. We still use our own language, our practices, and the context of the practices is African, every step of the way. And there is never the need or requirement to have anything else introduced into those religious practices and processes."

Undeniably, a cultural, religious, and racial fusion took place in Cuba, and a syncretic population was born. "In Cuba, dominated by the Catholic Church as it was, it made sense to function that way. In Nigeria each deity in a community has a temple." Pichardo further explained: "Apart from home worship, you have these centers. Ordination to the priesthood there is a community event. When slaves were brought to Cuba, their religion was outlawed by the Catholic Church. It had to be practiced clandestinely, and, yes, it became a way to deal with crisis."

Nonetheless, Pichardo adamantly insisted that "the *orishas* don't even classify as being equivalent to what is a saint. That doesn't even work. In fact, the concept of martyrs isn't even there, or is gray." The Lukumi's *orishas* and religious practices are polytheistic, like the *kami* (gods) of Shinto, not monotheistic like Christianity, Judaism, or Islam. Although there is a single god-creator of the universe, Olodumare is not idolized or considered a prophet.

"People are syncretic. The religion is not syncretic," Pichardo argues. "There are religions that are syncretic, but this one in particular is not." He takes strong exception with *santeros* and scholars who contend that Santeria was "born" in Cuba. "What was born in Cuba?" he says provocatively. "Cubans? I thought this religion was born in Africa!"

Some *santeros* and scholars disagreed. As Brandon explained:

The African religious system could not be reconstituted in its original form because memory of it was reshaped by the activities and experience of later generations of Afro-Cubans, slave and free, in the diverse contexts of Cuban society in which they found themselves. . . . For at least some people the old meanings remain the primary ones, the only ones which are truly correct. For others the old meaning becomes one of an array of possible alternative meanings. And for others the old and the new meanings are fused under a broader conception.

Another problem with portraying Santeria as a syncretic religion arises from the presumption that historically the Lukumi religion and Catholicism were each coherent and uniform. Moreover, the historical merger of Lukumi religious practices and folk Catholicism was neither uniform nor consistent. In Brandon's words:

People assimilated and retained Yoruba religion and Catholicism in different ways and at different rates as well as within different social and ecological situations so that there inevitably arose a range of variation. . . . Folk Catholics, church Catholics, people who practiced the different African religions at home and went to church, people who practiced mixed Afro-Cuban rites exclusively, as well as those who went to church and practiced Espiritismo, or Afro-Catholic-Spiritist religion, all claimed to be Catholic. The semantic content of the term *Catholic* thus became both rich and internally inconsistent.

Pichardo agreed that a lot of Cubans do not see a contradiction between Catholicism and Santeria. "With Catholicism you are told to pray and then wait. We, on the other hand, confront the crisis. We give people tools to fight these negative events in their lives. Those tools are the rites designed to bring back a spouse, solve work problems, or to save a dying relative. What we do is demonstrable. It is not based on faith."

The Cuban community in Hialeah and elsewhere remained divided. "Because Santeria was brought to Cuba by African slaves, many Cubans view it as backward, as a religion for the poor and uneducated," explained Lisandro Perez, a Cuban-born sociologist at Florida International University. Consequently, when the Church of the Lukumi announced plans to open to the public, controversy inexorably erupted, due in part to "fear that Santeria gives Cubans a bad public image, that it provides the potential for public embarrassment." Those fears were compounded by the fact that the political establishment and longtime residents of Hialeah were largely white Cubans who had arrived in the 1960s, whereas the Mariel boatlift had inundated South Florida with black Cubans from a lower socioeconomic class. Thus, opposition to the Church of the Lukumi was based in no small part on racial and class bias within the Cuban community.

Establishing a Church, Inflaming a Community

In the spring of 1987, the Church of the Lukumi announced plans to open the first public Santeria church in an abandoned used-car dealership at the corner of West Fifth Street and Okeechobee Road. This is a busy thoroughfare running along the Miami River. It is also only a couple of blocks from Hialeah's main street and city hall. In the neighborhood are several Catholic, Baptist, Pentecostal, and Evangelical churches, along with a number of *botanicas* (stores that sell herbs and other Santeria paraphernalia). Hialeah is no bedroom community; it is a working-class community of Cubans and Hispanics living in small houses and old apartments in an industrial city known largely for its famous racetrack with 400 pink flamingos.

The run-down building was badly in need of repair, but Ernesto and Fernando Pichardo had very ambitious plans. Besides providing a home for the church, they aimed to establish a theological school and a museum to display artifacts and paraphernalia of the Lukumi religion. They planned to conduct various religious ceremonies there, including animal sacrifices and Espiritismo séances, and to provide counseling. In addition, they initially wanted to have a day-care center and a food bank in the back of the building, where they would distribute prepared meals to the homeless.

The Pichardo brothers negotiated a lease with an option to buy the property and transfer it to the church. They undertook the project with their family's money and took possession of the property on April 1, 1987. Ernesto Pichardo made a $100 deposit for water and sewage service and another $200 deposit for electricity. In order to operate, the city required a certificate of the church's incorporation; proof of its tax-exempt status, which turned out to be unnecessary; and time to verify that the area was zoned for churches, which it was. The city also required an inspection of the property before issuing an occupancy permit. The Pichardos considered much of this harassment, but matters quickly grew worse.

Shortly after the church announced plans to open, it began to get publicity in the local newspapers, and angry protests started. About that time, in anticipation of the problems to come, Jorge A. Duarte offered his legal services to Pichardo and the church. He had met Ernesto Pichardo through his sister, a reporter for the *Miami Herald* who had written several articles on Santeria and the problems attributed to the recent arrivals from the Mariel boatlift. She and Pichardo had become friends, once traveling together to visit the Oyotunji African Village. The church had little money, and as the protests grew, Duarte's advice and legal representation became increasingly important.

Duarte, a Cuban Catholic who converted to Buddhism, had grown up in Coral Cables. In his youth, he became committed to defending civil rights and liberties. After graduating from the local community college, he studied political science, earning his bachelor's degree at the State University of New York at Stony Brook. He then went to Antioch School of Law in Washington, D.C. In the 1970s, Antioch, under the leadership of Edgar Cahn and his wife, was identified with liberal causes growing out the 1960s civil rights movement and was known for recruiting minorities and women committed to public-interest law. After graduating, Duarte worked for Miami-Dade County under Janet Reno and later formed his own law firm, Duarte Hess.

Duarte became Pichardo's and the church's principal attorney. He argued their case against Hialeah in the federal district court in Miami and pursued it to the Court of Appeals for the Eleventh Circuit and, ultimately, to the Supreme Court. He also proved instrumental in getting the support of the Miami chapter of the American Civil Liberties Union (ACLU) for the church's fight against Hialeah's ordinances banning ritual animal sacrifice.

———

Almost immediately after securing the lease, the church began, in Pichardo's words, "its public relations campaign." Pictures of what the renovated building would eventually look like were displayed. In a preopening announcement for the church, which at the time had about 300 members, politicians, academics, and members of the Santeria community were invited to attend. That only intensified opposition.

Alden S. Tarte, a Miami lawyer representing several neighbors, claimed that "thousands of people" were petitioning the city council to keep the church out of Hialeah because of its practice of animal sacrifice. In his view, "Santeria is not a religion. It is a throwback to the dark ages. It is a cannibalistic, Voodoo-like sect which attracts the worst elements of society, people who mutilate animals in a crude and most inhumane manner." Years later he stood firm. "The neighborhood went ape." he said. "Ernesto Pichardo is not the kind of guy you'd want next door." But Pichardo countered in the press: "We are just like any other religion and have the same constitutional rights."

Members of the Ecclesiastical Board of Hialeah, an interdenominational group, vigorously opposed the Church of the Lukumi from the outset. "We are not against freedom of speech or worship," insisted the Reverend Edwin Diaz of the Joreb Baptist Church. "But that there are still people in this era, in our civilized society of the United States, still sacrificing animals in religious rituals is indefensible and repugnant."

Julio Fernandez, a fundamentalist pastor at the Fe Para Miami Church, conceded that he had once practiced Santeria. "I've seen lawyers, doctors, and professionals do it," he lamented. "But mostly it's the uneducated. We pray for their conversion to Christianity and we pray for authorities to have the power not to allow the animal sacrifice. It's black magic, a cult." Diaz, among others on the Ecclesiastical Board, agreed. "This is not a question of freedom of religion. It's a question of civilized behavior."

The Roman Catholic Archdiocese of Miami did not oppose the Church of the Lukumi. However, it was concerned about Santeria's attraction for large numbers of Cuban and Hispanic immigrants, especially low-income families. In the words of the Most Reverend Eduardo Boza Masvidal: "We are witnessing a phenomenon among the Cuban population in exile which deeply concerns those of us who wish to see a truly Christian Cuban people. I refer to the rapid growth of 'Santeria' and of religious syncretism, particularly in Miami, New York, and New Jersey, to the extent that 'Santeria' has been officially admitted as a religion with the same rights as other religions in some areas of the United States."

Catholicism and Santeria are irreconcilable, Monsignor Boza stressed, because the latter is polytheistic. "Our attitude toward those who practice 'Santeria' should not be complete rejection, but rather an invitation to reflection and purification of the faith." He also warned of the "commercial exploitation" of believers by *botanicas*, the stores selling herbs, beads, and statues of saints and spirits, which he claimed were overcharging. Monsignor Boza also undoubtedly disapproved of parishioners turning to *santeros* instead of Catholic priests for counseling and problem solving.

The U.S. Conference of Catholic Bishops came out more strongly in opposition. In 1986, it appointed the Reverend James Lebar to study Santeria, and he made the conference's opposition clear: "Their practices violate our prescribed liturgy. We simply cannot accept people cutting off chickens' heads and associating themselves with the Catholic Church."

Many *santeros* took strong exception to the position of the Conference of Catholic Bishops. A *babalawo* who identified himself only as Manuel recalled the history of Catholicism in Cuba and of Christianity itself in his counterargument: "Sacrifices date back to the time of Christ, and they have been an intimate part of the [Catholic] church for centuries. For them to tell us it is pagan is hypocritical."

But Lebar maintained that the death of Jesus Christ was the final sacrifice. "What they are doing is witchcraft, not Catholicism." Still, Manuel and other followers of Santeria remained resolute: "It is easy for people who know nothing about Santeria to dismiss it as magic. And some of it is magic. But it is more than that, it is the spirit of Christ and the African gods. It is to help people. Is that evil or wicked?"

———

A few days after a preopening event for the Church of the Lukumi, the Hialeah city council held a public meeting on the growing controversy. Notably, a majority of the city council was Catholic, but not all the Cuban members were Catholic. The seven-member council consisted of Silvio Cardoso, Salvatore D'Angelo, Herman Echevarria, Julio Martinez, Andres Mejides, Paulino Nunez, and Ray Robinson; also present was Hialeah's popular but controversial mayor, Raul Martinez. Not one member of the council defended the Church of the Lukumi or its claim to the free exercise of religion.

Somewhat surprisingly, Ernesto Pichardo viewed the controversy and the city council's eventual action as politically motivated and having little to do with religion. In retrospect, he claimed that religious passions had been stirred and manipulated by Hialeah's politicians, particularly Mayor Martinez, during an election year, as much as by the outpouring of opposition from neighbors.

Prior to the announcement of the church's opening, recalled Pichardo, Santeria had encountered little opposition. There were several *botanicas* within blocks of the church and within walking distance from Hialeah's city hall. Admittedly, health officials expressed concern about the disposal of animal carcasses, and many law enforcement officials remained convinced that Santeria was connected with crime and drug dealing. Still, there had been no personal attacks or public outcry over the Church of the Lukumi. Moreover, Mayor Martinez, a Catholic, was rumored (and thought by Pichardo and Duarte) to practice Santeria.

Basically, Pichardo contended, Hialeah became embroiled over bitter campaigns for and against Mayor Martinez's reelection. His opponent was a friend of the owner of the church property, and he had a long-standing "blood feud" with the mayor. Republican candidate Nilo Juri ran against Martinez four times in the 1980s and early 1990s. In Pichardo's view, the underlying opposition to the church stemmed from efforts of the mayor's supporters to thwart any commercial use of the former used-car lot and thereby drive the owner out of Hialeah.

Whether or not the controversy was rooted in a bitter political battle between the mayor and his opponents, it is true that Mayor Martinez was under investigation by the Federal Bureau of Investigation (FBI) and was prosecuted several times for taking kickbacks from deals involving zoning and land development. Born in Cuba, Martinez had immigrated to Florida in 1960. He was a real estate broker and publisher of a Spanish-language weekly, *El Sol de Hialeah*, before entering politics. In 1981, at age thirty-two, he was elected mayor on a campaign to purge the city of dirty politics. But he quickly earned a reputation as "the biggest knuckle-dragger in Hialeah."

By the late 1980s, federal prosecutors were moving toward prosecuting Mayor Martinez. His first prosecution resulted in a conviction on six counts of extortion and racketeering, but the conviction was overturned because of flawed jury instructions and juror misconduct. Rumors and accusations continued to follow the mayor throughout the 1990s. A second trial ended with a hung jury in 1996. A third trial ended with the jury acquitting Mayor Martinez on one conspiracy charge but deadlocked on five other charges. Throughout it all he remained popular, winning landslide reelection.

Regardless of whether Mayor Martinez instigated the controversy or simply responded to pressure from local churches and residents for action against the Church of the Lukumi, his opponents also rallied their supporters against the church. The outpouring of opposition was, Ernesto conceded, "politically created by local churches and politicians pulling together." Sunday sermons denounced the church. Death threats began arriving in the mail. Protesters at the church's preopening events carried signs reading "Jesus Up, Satan Down." The church and what it represented were easy targets for local politicians in an election year.

Confronting Animal Rights

Another force was no less aggressive in pressing for a ban on ritual animal sacrifice, namely, animal rights groups. Pichardo had confronted them before when intervening in disputes between *santeros* and humane society officials over animal cruelty laws, but he underestimated their new aggressiveness. Nor did he fully appreciate that his eventual lawsuit against Hialeah would bring to the Supreme Court the first major confrontation between animal rights advocates and defenders of religious freedom.

Coincidentally, in the 1980s, the animal rights movement became more assertive, even though concerns about animal cruelty had originated more than a century earlier in England. The utilitarian philosopher and legal reformer Jeremy Bentham had promoted the view that animals are sentient beings capable of pain and suffering in an oft-quoted passage: "But a full grown horse or dog is beyond comparison a more rational as well as a more conversable animal than an infant of a day or a week or even a month old. But suppose they were otherwise. What would it avail? The question is not, can they reason? But can they suffer?" In 1822, Parliament passed the first law against cruelty to farm animals. Two years later, the Society for the Prevention of Cruelty to Animals (SPCA) was founded to lobby for further legislation. In 1892, Henry Salt, founder of the Humanitarian League, published his book *Animal Rights*, setting forth many of the arguments that influenced later developments.

In the United States, the movement lagged somewhat behind. In 1866, Henry Bergh founded the American Society for the Prevention of Cruelty to Animals (ASPCA), which pushed the passage of the first animal cruelty laws. Its law enforcement department became a model for ASPCA offices throughout the country, with agents empowered to issue summonses to individuals accused of committing misdemeanors. In 1870, the Washington Humane Society, the oldest and only congressionally chartered animal welfare organization, was founded to enforce anti-cruelty laws in the District of Columbia.

These early animal welfare organizations focused primarily on the passage of carriage laws — laws aimed at the abusive treatment of carriage horses by drivers. When motor vehicles replaced horse-drawn carriages in the early part of the twentieth century, they turned their attention to the urban problems of animal overpopulation, fighting for leash laws and promoting animal shelters.

In the 1950s, a number of these humane societies split apart, and new organizations formed. They focused attention on the treatment of animals in scientific research and in the entertainment industry. The Animal Welfare Institute was established in 1951 to bring attention to the treatment of laboratory animals. In 1954, members of the American Humane Association broke away to form the Humane Society of the United States (HSUS), which is now the world's largest animal protection organization, with ten regional offices, four affiliates, and approximately 7 million members.

The HSUS and other organizations founded in the 1950s moved beyond their focus on individual behavior and lobbied for legislation aimed at changing institutional behavior. As a result, Congress enacted the Humane Slaughter Act in 1958, requiring anesthesia or the stunning of animals prior to slaughter, but allowing exceptions for the religious slaughter of animals according to the Jewish and Islamic faiths. After a widely publicized HSUS and Maryland state police raid on a dog dealer who sold stray dogs to research laboratories, Congress passed the Laboratory Animal Welfare Act of 1966.

By the late 1970s and 1980s, the modern animal rights movement was emerging as a new moral and legal crusade. Changes in the movement's philosophy and tactics were influenced by the successes of the civil rights movement and the emergence of the women's movement. Philosopher Peter Singer's 1975 book *Animal Liberation* became the bible for a new generation of animal rights activists and groups. Inspired by Singer's book, Henry Spira staged a widely publicized protest in 1980 in New York City against the giant cosmetics company Revlon. His protest against Revlon's use of rabbits to test the safety of new products forced it to abandon such testing.

In 1980, college student Alex Pacheco and Ingrid Newkirk founded the People for the Ethical Treatment of Animals (PETA). It employed much more aggressive rhetoric and tactics than older animal rights groups had used. In 1981, PETA's undercover investigations resulted in the so-called Silver Spring monkeys case. For the first time, a research laboratory, the Institute for Behavioral Research in Silver Spring, Maryland, was convicted of cruelty to animals used in its experiments. PETA also gained public attention for staging protests at the National Institutes of Health, foreign embassies, and private laboratories, as well as for its animal liberations.

Even more fundamentalist animal rights groups began to emerge. Whereas Singer advanced utilitarian arguments for the ethical treatment of animals, another philosopher, Tom Regan, championed moral arguments based on the inherent worth of animals as living creatures. Inspired by his philosophy, some fundamentalist groups took more militant stances, including illegal actions such as breaking into and destroying laboratories that conducted animal experiments. The Animal Liberation Front, a British import, was designated a terrorist organization by the FBI for its destruction of laboratories during the liberation of animals.

Not surprisingly, practitioners of Santeria and advocates of animal rights increasingly came into conflict. There were confrontations around the country over *santeros'* violation of animal cruelty laws. Some backed down under pressure, agreeing to use wine instead of the blood of animals in rituals. Others negotiated compromises over their treatment of animals. In one case, *santeros* in New York sued, arguing that ritual animal sacrifice was protected by the First Amendment guarantee of religious freedom. In 1987, however, New York state courts rejected that claim in *First Church of Chango, Inc. v. American Society for Prevention of Cruelty to Animals*. Nevertheless, such actions in and out of court emboldened animal rights advocates.

As soon as the controversy over the Church of the Lukumi erupted, the regional office of the HSUS intervened. It urged Hialeah's city council to enact a law banning ritual animal sacrifices. At the time, the HSUS was lobbying city councils nationwide to pass a model ordinance criminalizing ritual animal sacrifice. Its model ordinance went beyond the ones Hialeah enacted, proposing penalties of up to six months in jail and a $1,000 fine for anyone convicted of ritual animal sacrifice.

Hialeah Bans Ritual Animal Sacrifice

On May 21, 1987, Florida Power and Light served written notice to the church that electric service would be discontinued if a certificate of occupancy was not obtained. The real spark came, however, when Pichardo's mother and other members of the church held an Espiritismo mass — not a Santeria rite, and one not uncommon for Cubans. The church decided to do so, in Pichardo's words, "as part of our marketing campaign to draw people in."

The certificate of occupancy had not been obtained because the property still had to pass the city's zoning inspection. So the mass, like other preopening events, would have to be held outside. But as people began to set up for the mass, a Florida Power and Light truck arrived. Workers went right to the electric meter and tore it from the wall. They claimed that the electricity had been improperly turned on in the first place. The driver also told Ernesto Pichardo that city officials had told him to stop the service, although city attorneys later vehemently denied this.

It was only one of many incidents that Pichardo considered a pattern of harassment by city employees. Garbage service was discontinued, even though a deposit had been made. Next, the water was cut off. Pichardo and the church undoubtedly fueled the controversy by holding preopening events outside at the former used-car lot. And the publicity in the press only further antagonized opponents.

Subsequently, the director of the city's office of code enforcement showed up at the church on Wednesday, May 27. He told Pichardo that the church was "breaking the law" by operating without an occupancy permit. Pichardo countered that since the church had not formally opened, it was not breaking the law. But the inspector insisted, and Pichardo finally agreed to apply for an occupancy permit. Pichardo and the inspector drove together to city hall to fill out the application, but it could not be completed because of all the signatures needed. Two days later, on Friday, May 29, Pichardo filed the completed form. Notably, no mention was made of the church's intention to publicly sacrifice animals on the property.

On the following Monday, June 1, the code inspectors returned. They found fire code violations, electrical problems (old wiring had not been removed), and a problem with the air-conditioning. They also claimed that there were inadequate bathroom facilities: there had to be two bathrooms, one for males and one for females, if the building was open to the public.

———

A week later, on Tuesday night, June 9, the Hialeah city council held a public meeting on the propriety of allowing the church to use the land as a place of worship. Three hours of hostile protests and angry denunciations followed in what Pichardo and others described as a "mob atmosphere." Members of the Ecclesiastical Board of Hialeah decried animal sacrifice as "barbaric," "medieval," and "satanic." The church was denounced as a "regress into paganism." There were also plenty of angry racial epithets.

"This is something out of the fifteenth century," council member Julio Martinez shouted to wide applause. Even in pre-Castro Cuba, he continued, "people were put in jail for practicing this religion. If we could not practice this [religion] in our homeland, why bring it to this country?"

Council member Andres Mejides agreed. Though defending the Jewish practice of kosher slaughtering on the grounds that it had a "real purpose," he condemned Santeria's ritual animal sacrifice. He was "totally against the sacrificing of animals. The Bible says we are allowed to sacrifice an animal for consumption, but not for any other purpose. I don't believe that the Bible allows that." More impassioned than reasoned, Mejides and many of the other speakers drew loud applause, even though their arguments were confused and confusing.

Numerous other people in the audience of about 300 vented their outrage over Santeria. They told of finding animal remains in public streets and parks and floating in the Miami River. One woman, Pat Keller, recounted her distress over living next door to a house where Santeria was practiced. "My nights were a horror of drums beating and animals screaming. I have seen them drink blood."

When Pichardo appeared briefly, he was booed, jeered, and denounced as "Satan," "the anti-Christ." He tried to counter that claims like Ms. Keller's were ridiculous and gross exaggerations, but he was repeatedly interrupted and taunted. Even if the city council stopped the church from getting the occupancy permit, he shot back, Hialeah was "not going to stop 50,000 from practicing [animal sacrifice]. It's going to continue inside homes."

Santeria is a "sin," "foolishness," "an abomination to the Lord," responded the chaplain of Hialeah's police department. *Santeros* worship "demons. We need to be helping people and sharing with them the truth that is found in Jesus Christ," he pleaded to the obviously sympathetic city council. "We would exhort you not to permit this church to exist."

The outrage of the frustrated and furious crowd escalated when city attorneys told council members that they could not legally stop the Church of the Lukumi from opening. "Gentlemen," said city attorney Bill Wetzel, "we cannot stop them from opening a church." Their religious beliefs are guaranteed by the First Amendment, he told them.

Assistant city attorney Richard Gross agreed. "They," he tried to say amid boos and hisses, "they, the same as any other religious group, have the right . . ." But he was cut off by angry shouting. "We don't want it. We don't want it. We don't want it," the crowd shouted, drowning him out.

"Hogwash, Mr. Gross," retorted council member Silvio Cardoso, drawing more cheers. "They are in violation of everything this country stands for. I believe this council has the authority to stop these people."

Attorneys Wetzel and Gross warned Mayor Martinez and the council that they could be held personally liable if they enacted a law discriminating against a particular religion in violation of the First Amendment. Under Section 1983 of the U.S. Code, government officials can be sued and held personally liable for violating individuals' constitutional rights.

Their warning gave the council pause. Yet when city council president Herman Echevarria asked, "What can we do to prevent the church from opening?" attorneys Wetzel and Gross had an answer. They claimed that passage of a proposed resolution, Resolution 87-66, would make it crystal clear that "this community will not tolerate religious practices which are abhorrent to its citizens."

That night, the council ultimately decided to table a proposed law and a vote on banning ritual animal sacrifice. Instead, the council unanimously passed an emergency ordinance incorporating the state's animal cruelty law as City Ordinance 87-40 and passed a resolution expressing concern about animal sacrifice and condemning animal cruelty. Florida's state animal cruelty law provided, "Whoever unnecessarily overloads, overdrives, tortures, torments, deprives of necessary sustenance or shelter, or unnecessarily or cruelly beats, mutilates, or kills any animal, or causes the same to be done, or carries in or upon any vehicle, or otherwise, any animal in a cruel or inhuman manner, is guilty of a misdemeanor of the first degree."

Resolution 87-66 unambiguously expressed the "concern that certain religions may propose to engage in practices which are inconsistent with public morals, peace or safety, and . . . that religious freedom shall not justify practices inconsistent with public morals, peace or safety." If that were not enough, the resolution reiterated the city's "commitment to a prohibition against any and all acts of any and all religious groups which are inconsistent with public morals, peace or safety."

As members of the council cast their votes, the audience cheered. Those in attendance mistakenly thought that the council was voting to ban ritual animal sacrifice. However, the state law superseded the city's ordinance, and it did not bar the practice of killing animals humanely, plus it specifically exempted slaughterhouses and the religious slaughtering of animals. In the view of Hialeah's city attorneys, the vote on the resolution was legally meaningless. When asked why the city council passed the measure, Gross replied simply, "Well, they made the crowd happy."

———

The controversy was not over. Rallies against the church continued, and pressure on the city council grew. The council decided to seek an advisory opinion from the state attorney general, Bob Butterworth, about the scope of the state's animal cruelty law and the city's legal options. Specifically, city attorney Wetzel requested an opinion about whether the state's law against animal cruelty prohibited "a religious group from sacrificing an animal in a religious ritual or practice" and whether Hialeah could enact ordinances "making religious animal sacrifice unlawful."

In the meantime, to bring the property up to code, Pichardo faced more costs and had difficulty finding electricians and plumbers to correct the problems. Not until July 7 was an electrician found and a permit obtained to make the new electrical installations. Those improvements were made, and the property passed electrical inspection on July 13.

As it happened, on Monday, July 13, Butterworth issued his advisory opinion, which emboldened Hialeah's city council, defenders of animal rights, and other opponents of the church. Butterworth interpreted the state animal cruelty law to bar ritual animal sacrifice unless the animal was to be eaten. In his words, "ritual sacrifice of animals for purposes other than food consumption" was not a "necessary" killing like hunting and fishing. Ritual animal sacrifice was "unnecessary," in the sense that such killings are "done without any useful motive, in the spirit of wanton cruelty or for the mere pleasure of destruction without in any sense [being] beneficial or useful to the person killing the animal."

Butterworth concluded that Santeria's practice of animal sacrifice violated Florida's animal cruelty law, in spite of the fact that most ritually sacrificed animals are eaten. If Hialeah passed an ordinance prohibiting ritual animal sacrifice, it would not conflict with state law. That was also the position of animal rights advocates in Tallahassee, although some wanted to impose additional restrictions on kosher slaughterhouses. State law and the federal Humane Slaughter Act of 1958 exempt the ritual slaughter of animals for religious purposes, such as *shehitah*, the kosher slaughtering of animals according to Jewish law.

Even though Butterworth's advisory opinion fell short of the position of some animal rights advocates, it clearly empowered Hialeah's city council and put the church on notice that its practices might be outlawed. City attorney Wetzel now told the press: "The city will do and act accordingly in the event that it is determined that laws have been broken and are consistently broken. Then, of course, the city will take appropriate action."

Duarte took strong exception to the state attorney general's opinion and advised Pichardo not "to curtail his religious practices." Pichardo pressed ahead, making the required improvements and planning for the formal opening of the church. He also provocatively told reporters that it was "quite possible" that some small animals, such as chickens, would be sacrificed at the activation service for the church. That only tantalized the press and further antagonized opponents.

Finding a plumber proved to be the most difficult part of repairing the building. Most plumbers were reluctant or refused to work on the property because of the controversy over the church. Some feared reprisals from city officials. Finally, a *santero* who was a plumber agreed to put in a second bathroom. He obtained the necessary permit on July 29 and made the addition. On August 3, the permit, detailing the improvements, was filed with the city. The next day, the plumbing inspectors arrived, and two days later, on August 6, a final inspection of the property was made.

About this time, Duarte met with Mayor Martinez. The mayor finally agreed that if the second bathroom was put in, he would "back off." He also guaranteed a certificate of occupancy. But he stood firm about not permitting animal sacrifice there. By this time, he probably could not have done otherwise, even if so inclined. The controversy was simply too hot.

The church finally received its certificate of occupancy on Friday, August 7. Two days later, on Sunday, August 9, it held an open house in celebration of what was proclaimed to be the country's first Santeria church. There was chanting, drum beating, and ceremonies with food, but no animals were sacrificed. About 150 people attended. A police perimeter was set up, but only a handful of picketers showed up.

The opening of the Church of the Lukumi was, in Pichardo's view, a historic event. "This Afro-Cuban religion has been repressed for 470 years," he told the crowd. "It was now coming out to be publicly recognized." However, the publicity and press coverage further embittered opponents and moved Hialeah's city council to enact ordinances making ritual animal sacrifice a crime.

———

Four days later, on August 11, Hialeah's city council adopted another resolution reaffirming "the policy of the Mayor and City Council of the City of Hialeah, Florida, to oppose the ritual sacrifices of animals within the City of Hialeah, Florida." It also stated unambiguously: "Any individual or organization that seeks to practice animal sacrifice in violation of state and local law will be prosecuted."

In September, the city council adopted three more ordinances. On September 8, it enacted Ordinance 87-52, prohibiting the possession of animals intended for sacrifice or slaughter. It was apparently aimed at *botanicas* that sold small animals and other paraphernalia used in Santeria rites. On September 22, the two other ordinances were enacted. Ordinance 87-71 expressly prohibited the ritual sacrifice of animals, and Ordinance 87-72 prohibited the slaughter of animals on premises not expressly zoned for that purpose (these ordinances are reprinted in the appendix). All three ordinances were adopted unanimously. Violations of each were punishable by fines of up to $500, imprisonment of up to 60 days, or both.

The Church Fights Back

Pichardo and Duarte denounced the ordinances as discriminatory and a violation of the First Amendment's guarantee of religious freedom. "It's just a continuing process of religious persecution," Duarte told reporters. On September 25, three days after enactment of the last two ordinances and before any enforcement action could be threatened, Pichardo and the church filed a lawsuit in the U.S. District Court for the Southern District of Florida.

Actually, Pichardo and the church had filed a suit against Hialeah after the first resolutions were passed in June and August, seeking a declaratory judgment that they were unconstitutional. In addition, they sued each member of the city council and Mayor Martinez for "illegal, unconstitutional harassment, threats, and discrimination," as well as for misusing their offices in violation of the Constitution. They contended that the mayor and council members should be held personally liable under Section 1983 for "intervening and causing" police harassment of members of the church, the refusal by city employees to pick up garbage, and the cutting off of electricity by public employees.

Because of the complexity of the issues and because the church had little money, Duarte sought the support of a number of organizations, including the American Jewish Congress and the local chapter of the ACLU. They initially turned him down. Apparently, some ACLU lawyers were sympathetic to animal rights supporters. Others, according to Pichardo, really did not understand the case. "It took a lot of communication to get them aboard. This was not your typical ACLU case," he says in retrospect. In his view, the ACLU had "serious conflicts over the case" and treated the church as "this strange thing, this interesting case."

The Miami chapter of the ACLU took a second vote and agreed to provide assistance. It paid the basic expenses of the litigation, such as the cost of depositions of expert witnesses and transcripts. Two attorneys associated with the ACLU worked with Duarte in arguing the case in district court. Mitchell A. Horwich, an older and locally well-known attorney, argued primarily the First Amendment claims. Maurice Rosen focused on the issue of liability under Section 1983. As the lead attorney at the trial, Duarte provided the "big picture" of their challenge to Hialeah.

Hialeah was represented by Richard G. Garrett, a forty-one-year-old lawyer from a leading Miami law firm, Greenberg and Traurig. Garrett grew up in Miami Beach and later went to Emory University and its school of law in Atlanta, Georgia. After practicing law for a couple of years in Georgia, he moved back to Miami, where he specialized in litigation. Shortly after the resolutions and ordinances were challenged, lawyers for Hialeah interviewed him, along with others, and hired him to represent the city. At the trial, he was assisted by two other members of his firm, Stuart H. Singer and Laura T. Thomas.

Garrett countered that because the resolutions were legislative acts, the mayor and council members enjoyed full immunity. He contended that there was no evidence they had instructed the police or city workers to harass or infringe on the rights of Pichardo and the church. Garrett sought a summary judgment dismissing the suit. He also had the backing of the state attorney general. Michael J. Neiman of the Florida attorney general's office appeared before federal district court judge Eugene P. Spellman as a "friend of the court," even though no challenge had been made to the state law against animal cruelty.

The attempt to hold the mayor and city council liable failed. Judge Spellman dismissed the claims and separated the issue of liability from the constitutional challenge to Hialeah's resolutions and ordinances. On June 10, 1988, he ruled that Mayor Martinez and the city council had acted in their official capacities in enacting the resolutions. Under Supreme Court precedents on public officials' immunity from liability, he held that they were entitled to absolute immunity. In addition, Judge Spellman found no evidence that the police or other city officials had been directed to harass Pichardo or members of the church.

Years later, Duarte and Pichardo still maintain that the city harassed the church. At the time, though, Pichardo began to realize that opening the church had not served to educate or to eliminate misconceptions about the religion. "The issue of our beliefs and practices has been greatly exaggerated, especially by many of the mainstream religious people," he observed. "The attacks have scared away many worshippers. We have been forced into this lawsuit because it's our only way to survive."

The central constitutional issue of whether Hialeah's ordinances against ritual animal sacrifice violated the First Amendment remained and came into bold relief in the subsequent trial before Judge Spellman.

CHAPTER 3

Minorities and Religious Freedom

As Cuban immigrants and priests practicing a poorly understood minority religion, Ernesto Pichardo and the other founders of the Church of the Lukumi were in a sense quintessential Americans fighting for religious freedom. The country has absorbed waves of immigrants and religious minorities, many of whom had the courage of their convictions and took their constitutional rights seriously. The hard-fought struggles of religious minorities transformed religious freedom from a tradition of freedom *from* governmental endorsement of any particular religion into freedom *to* openly practice nonconformist religions.

The modern libertarian conception of religious freedom did not emerge until the early twentieth century, however. It was the result of the struggles of religious minorities such as the Church of Jesus Christ of Latter-day Saints (Mormons), Jehovah's Witnesses, Orthodox Jews, and others. It took decades and a series of (not always successful) lawsuits to persuade the Supreme Court and the country of the value of protecting individuals' free exercise of religion.

The Court nonetheless came to embrace this new theory of freedom. As Justice Lewis F. Powell observed in the important 1974 ruling on libel in *Gertz v. Robert Welch:* "Under the First Amendment there is no such thing as a false idea." In other words, under the First Amendment, there is no religious *truth*. The First Amendment relegates religious truths to matters of private opinion. Government may neither endorse or advance a particular religion nor ban or otherwise discriminate against religious beliefs and viewpoints. That was the principle at stake in *Church of the Lukumi Babalu Aye, Inc., and Ernesto Pichardo v. City of Hialeah.*

Religious Freedom and the Founding

Religious freedom is guaranteed in the two opening clauses of the First Amendment: "Congress shall make no law respecting an establishment of religion, or prohibiting the free exercise thereof." Together, they guarantee freedom from and of religion by pointing in opposite directions. The (dis)establishment clause points toward the principle of *separation of government from religion;* neither should involve itself with the other. The free exercise clause suggests a principle of *voluntarism* — freedom from governmental coercion in choosing a religion or no religion.

Neither the text nor the historical record of the amendment provides easy interpretive solutions for controversies arising over the scope of religious freedom. What is a "law respecting an establishment of religion"? What is and who defines "religion"? The framers were not of one mind. The Constitution, as Madison repeatedly reminded his contemporaries, "was not, like the fabled Goddess of Wisdom, the offspring of a single brain." He expressly rejected appeals to the framers' "original intent" as "a hard rule of construction" and even deemed the constitutional convention's debates to lack "authoritative character." Furthermore, many of the contemporary disputes over religious freedom were not foreseen. There was no controversy over school prayer or vouchers, for instance, because there was no system of public education. History thus often fails to answer questions about the protections of the First Amendment and other matters of constitutional interpretation.

The traditions and aspirations of religious freedom are also complex and often conflicting. Although populated by those escaping religious persecution in England and on the European continent, colonial settlements remained religious enclaves, discriminating against people of other faiths. In Massachusetts, the established Congregational Church taxed and harassed Quakers, Baptists, and others. In Virginia and four other southern colonies, the Anglican Church of England was established. "Colonial America," as political scientist John R. Roche observed, "was an open society dotted with closed enclaves, and one could generally settle in with his co-believers in safety and comfort and exercise the right of oppression."

As the colonies moved toward the Declaration of Independence in 1776, religious freedom began to take on new meaning, rejecting the European understanding of an established church-state. England, Scotland, and parts of Germany had established churches, and the Roman Catholic Church had been established in Italy, Spain, and elsewhere. But in 1774, when the English Parliament passed a statute establishing both Anglicanism and Catholicism in Canada, the Continental Congress protested with "astonishment, that a British Parliament should ever consent to establish in that country a religion that has deluged [England] in blood, and dispersed bigotry, persecution, murder and rebellion through every part of the world."

By the 1770s, the original thirteen colonies, always predominantly Protestant, were on their way to a new form of establishment, unlike the European single state-church denomination. Christianity or Protestantism was established in the northern colonies but allowed for multiple denominations. Four colonies (Rhode Island, Pennsylvania, Delaware, and New Jersey) never established a state religion. Virginia's Patrick Henry championed *nonpreferentialism*, that is, no governmental aid for any particular religion but support for all religions. Nonpreferentialism fell out of favor in the early nineteenth century, however, as states abandoned established churches and religious qualifications for holding state office.

Religious freedom also found expression in the Constitution. Article VI provides that "no religious Test shall ever be required as a Qualification to any Office or public Trust under the United States." That was not enough to silence critics pressing for the addition of a bill of rights. On June 12, 1788, during Virginia's ratifying convention, Madison sought to reassure those who feared governmental denial of religious freedom by explaining: "Happily for the states, they enjoy the utmost freedom of religion. This freedom arises from that multiplicity of sects, which pervades America, and which is the best and only security for religious liberty in any society. For where there is such a variety of sects, there cannot be a majority of any one sect to oppress and persecute the rest."

Madison failed to dissuade those demanding greater protection for religious freedom. When ratifying the Constitution, the Virginia convention proposed the addition of a bill of rights, including the following provision:

That religion or the duty which we owe to our Creator, and the manner of discharging it can be directed only by reason and conviction, not by force or violence, and therefore all men have an equal, natural and unalienable right to the free exercise of religion according to the dictates of conscience, and that no particular religious sect or society ought to be favored or established by Law in preference to others.

Subsequently, in the House of Representatives, Madison championed the constitutional amendments that resulted in the Bill of Rights. In addition, he sought to persuade the first Congress that the states, no less than the federal government, should be barred from passing laws respecting religious freedom. On June 8, 1789, he introduced a series of proposed amendments, including: "The civil rights of none shall be abridged on account of religious belief or worship, nor shall any national religion be established, nor shall the full and equal rights of conscience be in any manner, or on any pretext, infringed." Another stated: "No State shall violate the equal rights of conscience, or the freedom of the press, or the trial by jury in criminal cases."

Without debate, Madison's proposals were referred to a special committee. Within a week, it reported back to the full House. His proposals remained intact, except for some minor editing. The House then devoted a single day to considering what would become the First Amendment. As a result of a motion by Fisher Ames, the revised amendment read: "Congress shall make no law establishing religion, or prohibiting the free exercise thereof, nor shall the rights of conscience be infringed."

The House's proposed amendments were debated in secret in the Senate in September. The *Senate Journal*, however, records three unsuccessful motions to change the amendment on September 3. All would have narrowed the amendment to bar establishments preferring "one religious sect or society" or "any particular denomination of religion in preference to another." Six weeks later, the Senate voted to amend the House's version to read: "Congress shall make no law establishing articles of faith or a mode of worship, or prohibiting the free exercise of religion." This change narrowed the religion clauses to bar only the endorsement of a single denomination or national religion.

Under it, Congress could provide nondiscriminatory aid to all religions, something the Baptists bitterly opposed.

The Senate's changes provoked opposition in the House. A joint conference committee, chaired by Madison, was created to resolve their differences. On September 24, the House agreed to the Senate's version of other amendments on the condition that the provision for religious freedom be changed to its present form: "Congress shall make no laws respecting an establishment of religion, or prohibiting the free exercise thereof." The Senate agreed, and the amendment was adopted.

Madison's efforts to guarantee "the full and equal rights of conscience" and to forbid the states to violate "the equal rights of conscience" failed. States continued to sanction vestiges of establishment and restrictions on religious freedom. Massachusetts, for one, discriminated against religious minorities, denying Jews the right to hold public office until 1828; it did not remove its final vestiges of establishment until 1833.

Religious discrimination persisted throughout the nineteenth century, and the Supreme Court did little to enforce the First Amendment guarantee of the free exercise of religion. Not until 1940 in *Cantwell v. Connecticut* did the Court hold that the free exercise clause limited the states as well as the federal government. In that case, the Court struck down a permit requirement for soliciting funds on public streets that had been challenged by Jehovah's Witnesses, because their faith requires them to proselytize. Almost 150 years after the adoption of the Bill of Rights, the Court finally recognized that the free exercise of religion is a "fundamental right." Seven years later, the Court made the (dis)establishment clause applicable to the states in *Everson v. Board of Education*, in which Justice Hugo L. Black wrote the "high wall theory" of separation of government and religion into constitutional law.

With these rulings the Court ignited the ongoing debate over religious freedom and over its own role in enforcing the First Amendment. In doing so, the Court abandoned the older conception of religious freedom and gave birth to a contemporary conception and established the Court's role in defending religious minorities against discrimination.

Belief versus Action

The persistence of the older conception of religious freedom throughout the nineteenth century is evident in the Court's initial rulings on
the free exercise clause. In a series of cases, Mormons fought against
federal legislation outlawing and punishing the practice of polygamy,
from *Reynolds v. United States* (1878) to *Late Corporation of Church of
Jesus Christ of Latter Day Saints v. United States* (1890). These cases
resulted in the Court's elevating into constitutional law a central distinction — the distinction between *belief* and *action* — that would come
into play in Pichardo's suit against Hialeah.

There was no more vilified religious minority in the nineteenth
century than the Mormons. In the 1830s, because of hostility in New
York and elsewhere in the East, they fled to the Midwest. In Illinois,
Joseph Smith, the church's founder, added fuel to the fire of controversy by introducing several new doctrines, including the practice of
polygamy. In order to escape continued persecution, his successor,
Brigham Young, led the Mormons farther west to the Great Salt Lake
basin. Polygamy was publicly embraced at a church conference in
1852, resulting in even greater hostility from mainline Protestant religions. Every state outlawed polygamy, and public demand grew for
federal legislation banning polygamy in the territories.

Between 1862 and 1887, Congress enacted a series of statutes outlawing polygamy, forbidding polygamists to serve on juries and vote
in federal elections, and eventually disincorporating the Mormon
Church. Mormons refused to yield. In Utah, the territorial legislature
fought back by expressly sanctioning polygamy. In 1860, the House of
Representatives responded by passing a bill outlawing polygamy in the
territories. It was controversial, but only because of doubt about congressional authority over the territories. This doubt was due to the
infamous 1857 ruling in *Dred Scott v. Sandford*, invalidating the Mis-
souri Compromise of 1820 and holding that Congress lacked the
power to prohibit slavery in territories north of the 36°31′ line. Two
more years passed before Congress enacted the Anti-Polygamy Acts
of 1862.

Congress did not deem its legislation making polygamy a crime, punishable by a fine of up to $500 and a prison term of up to five years, to be discriminatory. Rather, it was aimed at promoting civilized, decent, and moral behavior. Nor did Congress consider it an infringement on the right "to worship God according to the dictates of conscience." Congress drew on the distinction between belief and action that Thomas Jefferson had championed in his Bill for Establishing Religious Freedom. There, he observed that "the acts of the body, unlike the operations of the mind, are subject to the coercion of the laws."

When it upheld the prohibition on polygamy in *Reynolds v. United States*, the Court wrote Jefferson's distinction into constitutional law. In Chief Justice Morrison Waite's words, it marked "the true distinction between what properly belongs to the church and what to the State." He neither questioned the need to force religious minorities to conform to the will of the majority nor thought much about the Court's enforcement of the free exercise clause to protect religious minorities.

The distinction between belief and action became a central pillar in the Court's subsequent application of the free exercise clause. The First Amendment, as Justice Owen Roberts observed in *Cantwell*, "embraces two concepts — freedom to believe and freedom to act. The first is absolute but, in the nature of things, the second cannot be. Conduct remains subject to regulation of society."

The distinction between belief and action reverberated in the case of the Church of the Lukumi. In defending Hialeah's ordinances, Garrett maintained that the city simply banned the practice of ritual animal sacrifice, not the belief in Santeria. Attorneys for animal rights groups supported Hialeah's ordinances as merely prohibiting animal cruelty without coercing or discriminating against religious belief. In the term before it heard oral arguments in the church's case, the Court upheld an airport's ban on solicitations while striking down its ban on the distribution of literature within the terminal, over the objections of followers of Krishna Consciousness, in *International Society for Krishna Consciousness, Inc. v. Lee* (1992). The Court had upheld a similar ordinance banning solicitations at a fairground more than a decade earlier in *Heffron v. International Society for Krishna Consciousness* (1981). It did so even though followers of Krishna Consciousness, somewhat like Jehovah's Witnesses, believe that they must distribute

{ *Animal Sacrifice and Religious Freedom* }

religious literature and solicit funds for their religion in public places, in a ritual known as *sankirtan*.

———

Protecting Religious Minorities

The Court's modern approach to the free exercise clause did not emerge until the 1940s, out of the battles of the Jehovah's Witnesses. They were easy targets due to their proselytizing, which is central to their faith and is based on their reading of the Bible. Matthew 24:14 states: "And this gospel of the kingdom will be preached throughout the whole world, as testament to all nations; and then the end will come." For the Witnesses, proselytizing is a labor of love. However, it also brought them into conflict with local laws forbidding door-to-door canvassing, soliciting without a permit, and even child labor laws.

Cantwell v. Connecticut was crucial in holding that the free exercise clause is incorporated into the Fourteenth Amendment's due process clause and is therefore a limitation on the states. In addition, the facts and the Court's analysis are illuminating about the emerging understanding of the free exercise clause and the Court's role in protecting religious minorities.

Newton Cantwell and his two sons, Jesse and Russell, had gone to a Catholic neighborhood in New Haven, Connecticut, to distribute *The Watchtower*. At some point, Jesse stopped two men, both Catholics. He asked them to listen to a recording about the Witnesses that contained a diatribe against the Catholic Church. The men became outraged and threatened him, whereupon the Cantwells left. Subsequently, they were prosecuted and convicted for breach of the peace. On appeal, they were represented by a fellow true believer and a courageous attorney, Hayden Covington. Between 1938 and 1955, he won over two dozen Witness cases before the Court, most of which were decided on free speech grounds instead of the free exercise clause. In *Lovell v. City of Griffin* (1938), for instance, the Court overturned as a prior restraint the conviction of Witness Alma Lovell for running afoul of an ordinance requiring handbill distributors to obtain permission from the city manager. A year later, *Schneider v. New Jersey* (1939) struck down another ordinance regulating the distribution of handbills.

In *Cantwell*, the Court might have upheld the conviction under the *Reynolds* distinction between belief and action. Under Connecticut law, soliciting without a license and breach of the peace were "actions which were in violation of social duties or subversive of good order." Instead, Justice Roberts undertook a more searching inquiry, balancing (rather than simply deferring to) the state's interests against the Witnesses' free exercise claim. He also equated religious freedom with freedom of speech. Here, censorship of religious speech could not be condoned, for it implicated a particular religion's very right to survive, as he put it, through "the solicitation of aid for the perpetuation of religious views or systems."

Unlike the state courts that had upheld Cantwell's conviction, the Supreme Court gave greater weight to the claim of religious freedom and did not deem Cantwell's conduct an incitement or breach of the peace. This was not a case of so-called fighting words, or unprotected speech, as the Court had found in another Witness case, *Chaplinsky v. New Hampshire* (1942). There, the Court had upheld the conviction of a Witness under a statute forbidding the use of offensive language in public. At the time of his arrest for creating a public disturbance, Walter Chaplinsky had called the arresting officer "a Goddamned racketeer" and "a damned Fascist." By contrast, Cantwell had been convicted only for trying "to persuade a willing listener to buy a book or to contribute money in the interest of what Cantwell, however misguided others may think him, conceived to be true religion."

Cantwell pointed toward a new understanding of the free exercise of religion. The Court would give such claims greater scrutiny. Particular religions could not be targeted in a discriminatory fashion, and the government must have a compelling state interest for overriding minorities' religious freedom.

Ironically, the struggles of the Jehovah's Witnesses expanded the First Amendment protection for all Americans, even though they were despised, contentious, anti-Catholic, and intolerant of others. In the 1940s, they were also considered un-American. A number of states had laws requiring schoolchildren to salute the American flag at the start of the school day, and the Witnesses refused. They contended that doing so violated the Bible's command not to bow down before a graven image. As a result, vigilantes in the Midwest and Texas tracked them down, broke up their meetings, and beat them, or worse. The wave of violence escalated in the spring of 1940 as the German army raced across Europe and Americans feared the Witnesses were in fact a subversive "Fifth Column" preparing for a Nazi invasion.

No less ironically, two weeks after *Cantwell* came down, the Court upheld a compulsory flag-salute statute in *Minersville School District v. Gobitis* (1940). Justice Felix Frankfurter — a Jewish immigrant from Austria and a prominent liberal professor at Harvard Law School before Franklin D. Roosevelt named him to the Court in 1939—delivered the opinion for the Court. He posed the conflict as simply one between governmental authority and personal liberty, not the higher duty of religious obligation. He also relied on a unanimous ruling upholding compulsory courses in military science over the objections of Jehovah's Witnesses in *Hamilton v. Regents of the University of California* (1934). In his view, religious minorities were not entitled to exemption from generally applicable laws. As he explained:

> The religious liberty which the Constitution protects has never excluded legislation of general scope not directed against doctrinal loyalties of particular sects. Judicial nullification of legislation cannot be justified by attributing to the framers of the Bill of Rights views for which there is no historic warrant. Conscientious scruples have not, in the course of the long struggle for religious toleration, relieved the individual from obedience to a general law not aimed at the promotion or restriction of religious beliefs.

Justice Harlan Fiske Stone — a former Columbia Law School professor appointed in 1925 by Calvin Coolidge — dissented. He adamantly challenged Justice Frankfurter's judicial self-restraint and deference to the will of democratically elected legislative majorities. In underscoring the importance of the Bill of Rights and the role of the Court as a guardian of those liberties, Justice Stone protested:

> The Constitution expresses more than the conviction of the people that democratic processes must be preserved at all costs. It is also an expression of faith and a command that freedom of the mind and spirit must be preserved, which government must obey, if it is to adhere to the justice and moderation without which no

free government can exist. For this reason it would seem that legislation which operates to repress the religious freedom of small minorities, which is admittedly within the scope of the protection of the Bill of Rights, must at least be subject to the same judicial scrutiny as legislation which we have recently held to infringe the constitutional liberty of religious and racial minorities.

The lineup in *Gobitis* was not exactly as it appeared. Three justices who joined the majority — Black, William O. Douglas, and Frank Murphy — immediately regretted it. Justice Douglas, a former Yale Law School professor named to the Court by FDR in 1939, later reflected that they had gone along because Justice Frankfurter was "learned in constitutional law and we were inclined to take him at face value." Justice Murphy, another FDR appointee, had arrived at the Court just a few months earlier and actually drafted a dissent but withheld it because he was new and deferential to Frankfurter.

Gobitis was excoriated in the press. The *New Republic*, which Justice Frankfurter had helped found when at Harvard, blasted the decision. It warned of the "great danger of adopting Hitler's philosophy [of repression] in the effort to oppose Hitler's legions." The American Civil Liberties Union (ACLU), which Frankfurter had also helped found, lamented in its 1941 report: "No religious organization has suffered such persecution since the days of the Mormons."

With the large number of Witness cases arriving at the Court's doorstep, Justices Black, Douglas, and Murphy soon found occasion to express their disagreement with *Gobitis*. Two years later in *Jones v. Opelika*, the justices split five to four in upholding Witnesses' conviction for proselytizing in violation of a license tax on the sale of printed materials. Stone had been elevated to chief justice in 1941, giving his dissent in *Opelika* added authority: "The First Amendment is not confined to safeguarding freedom of speech and freedom of religion against discriminatory attempts to wipe them out. On the contrary the Constitution, by virtue of the First and Fourteenth Amendments, has put these freedoms in a preferred position."

In a separate dissent, Justices Black, Douglas, and Murphy recanted their votes in *Gobitis*, explaining: "Since we joined the opinion in the *Gobitis* case, we think this is an appropriate occasion to state that we now believe that it was also wrongly decided. Certainly our democratic form of government functioning under the historic Bill of Rights has a high responsibility to accommodate itself to the religious views of minorities however unpopular and unorthodox those views may be. The First Amendment does not put the right freely to exercise religion in a subordinate position." Along with Chief Justice Stone, they set the stage for deciding a second flag-salute case.

Although not always prevailing, the Jehovah's Witnesses fought on. They were aided by the ACLU's championing their cause. In 1917, Roger Baldwin, a Bostonian aristocrat, had organized the Civil Liberties Bureau of the American Union Against Militarism to defend draft resisters during World War I. "Up until then," he recalled before his death in 1981, "there had been only scattered civil liberties movements [in the United States]. This was the first time the wholesale attack on civil liberties forced a nonpartisan defense of the principles of the Bill of Rights of a countrywide character." In 1920, that organization was reorganized as the ACLU, with local chapters nationwide.

Without exaggeration, the ACLU almost single-handedly invented the modern conception of civil rights and liberties through its championing of the causes of minorities such as the Jehovah's Witnesses. Much of what the ACLU accomplished was done through its attorneys, such as Horwich and Rosen of the ACLU's Miami chapter, who defended Pichardo and the church. However, through its nationwide confederation of local chapters, the ACLU also formulated a body of civil rights doctrine around which editors, ministers, teachers, unionists, and common citizens mobilized. For every card-carrying ACLU member, as Baldwin told John Roche, there were hundreds of nonmembers who looked to it for leadership and carried its views into communities around the country.

Among the ACLU's many successes were cases brought by the Witnesses, including the seminal ruling in *West Virginia State Board of Education v. Barnette* (1943), which overruled *Gobitis*. As in *Gobitis*, the ACLU's amicus curiae (friend of the court) brief hammered home its argument that compulsory flag-salute statutes infringed on the First Amendment's guarantee of free speech and religious freedom.

In *Barnette*, Chief Justice Stone could have chosen to write the Court's opinion, since he had dissented in *Gobitis* and chief justices tend to take major opinions for themselves. Instead, he assigned the opinion to Justice Robert H. Jackson, who had been FDR's attorney general before his elevation to the high bench in 1941. Justice Jackson proved to be one of the Court's most gifted writers. Here, basing the decision on the First Amendment as a whole, rather than just the free exercise clause, he eloquently explained:

> The very purpose of a Bill of Rights was to withdraw certain subjects from the vicissitudes of political controversy, to place them beyond the reach of majorities and officials and establish them as legal principles to be applied by the courts. One's right to life, liberty, and property, to free speech, a free press, freedom of worship and assembly, and other fundamental rights may not be submitted to vote; they depend on the outcome of no elections.

Since the First Amendment enjoys a "preferred position," heightened judicial scrutiny was required. Justice Jackson left little doubt that the Court had firmly embraced a new understanding of its role in enforcing the First Amendment. In his words:

> The right of a State to regulate, for example, a public utility may well include, so far as the due process test is concerned, power to impose all of the restrictions which a legislature may have a "rational basis" for adopting. But freedoms of speech and press, of assembly, and of worship may not be infringed on such slender grounds. They are susceptible of restriction only to prevent grave and immediate danger to interests which the state may lawfully protect.

Barnette was a watershed. Still, the Jehovah's Witnesses and the ACLU continued fighting, losing some cases but winning many more. The Court rejected their claim for a religious exemption from child labor laws that prohibited minors from selling newspapers on city streets in *Prince v. Massachusetts* (1944), for instance. However, *Murdock v. Commonwealth of Pennsylvania* (1943) struck down a licensing tax on public solicitations, *Martin v. Struthers* (1943) held that Witnesses may not be barred from proselytizing on Sundays, *Jamison v. Texas* (1943) struck down a statute barring handbill distribution as applied to the Witnesses, *Marsh v. Alabama* (1946) ruled that even a private company town may not ban the distribution of religious literature, and *Niemotko v. Maryland* (1951) held that Witnesses may not be denied the use of public parks.

As historian William Leuchtenburg observed, up until the 1950s, no group "more affected the course of civil liberties than the Jehovah's Witnesses." Their constitutional battles marked "the dawn of the rights revolution."

The Court's new appreciation for protecting religious freedom was soon put to another test in *United States v. Ballard* (1944). In *Ballard*, the justices reaffirmed that the principle of religious neutrality and nondiscrimination means that government may not judge the truth or falsity of religious beliefs. At issue was the prosecution of the leaders of the "I Am" religion for mail fraud. Guy Ballard, the founder of the religion, had claimed to be the messenger of Master Saint Germain and to have the power to cure diseases. His widow and son were charged with making claims about curing diseases that they knew to be false. But the Court held that at their trial, the jury could not determine the truth or falsity of their religious claims. The jury could decide only whether they sincerely believed their claims or were deceitful and guilty of misrepresentations. "Men may believe what they cannot prove." Justice Douglas observed: "They may not be put to the proof of their religious doctrines or beliefs. The First Amendment does not select any one group or any one type of religion for preferred treatment."

In sum, the government may prosecute religious leaders and their followers for crimes such as tax evasion, fraud, misrepresentation, or child abuse. But the government may not try to define *religion* or *religious truths*, for that inexorably runs the risk of discriminating against religious beliefs, which are absolutely protected under the First Amendment.

The Warren and Burger Courts

The Court under Chief Justice Earl Warren, a popular governor of California named by Republican Dwight D. Eisenhower to the high bench in 1953, pushed the rights revolution in new and controversial directions. The landmark school desegregation decision, *Brown v. Board of Education of Topeka, Kansas* (1954), legitimated the civil rights movement. *Baker v. Carr* (1962) inaugurated a "reapportionment revolution." In a series of rulings on the rights of the accused in the 1960s, the Warren Court forged a "due process revolution" with rulings such as *Mapp v. Ohio* (1961) on the Fourth Amendment exclusionary rule, *Miranda v. Arizona* (1966) on the Fifth Amendment guarantee against self-incrimination, and *Gideon v. Wainwright* (1963) on indigents and the Sixth Amendment right to counsel.

The Warren Court also ignited a continuing controversy over school prayer by striking down, as a violation of the (dis)establishment clause, the requirement that students recite nondenominational prayers, the Lord's Prayer, and Bible verses in, respectively, *Engel v. Vitale* (1962), *Abington School District v. Schempp* (1963), and *Murray v. Curlett* (1963). The Warren Court also reaffirmed the fundamental principle of state neutrality toward religion when it struck down a law requiring public officeholders to swear an oath declaring their belief in God in *Torcaso v. Watkins* (1961).

However, Chief Justice Warren upheld laws requiring businesses to close on Sundays — over the free exercise claims of Orthodox Jews, who observe the Sabbath on Saturday. They objected to being forced to close their businesses on Sundays as well. Splitting five to four in *Braunfeld v. Brown* (1961) and three companion cases, Chief Justice Warren commanded a bare majority in upholding the Sunday closing laws, although his opinion for the Court was joined by only a plurality.

In Chief Justice Warren's view, government had a legitimate interest in a generally applicable law ensuring workers a day of rest, and the burden on Orthodox Jews was only "indirect" and "incidental." By "indirect" he did not mean "insubstantial," for he stipulated that if Abraham Braunfeld's business remained closed on Saturdays and he was prevented from opening on Sundays, he would be "unable to continue in his business, thereby losing his capital investment." Pennsylvania's law was unquestionably costly for Orthodox Jews. Still, Chief Justice Warren emphasized that Braunfeld did not confront an unavoidable choice between following the dictates of his faith and complying with the law, even though at a very high price. Braunfeld did not face a "direct" burden on his religion, and the First Amendment principles of religious nondiscrimination and state neutrality bar only direct burdens. In contrast, indirect burdens render compliance with a law only more expensive or difficult.

Although *Braunfeld* appeared to treat religious minorities harshly, at least in the view of the dissenters, Chief Justice Warren emphasized that there was no question about the unconstitutionality of laws that directly target religious minorities. In his words: "If the purpose or effect of a law is to impede the observance of one or all religions or is to discriminate invidiously between religions, that law is constitutionally invalid even though the burden may be . . . only indirect."

Justice William Brennan, who usually sided with Chief Justice Warren, dissented. Two years later, he turned his dissent in *Braunfeld* into an opinion for the Court in *Sherbert v. Verner* (1963). Adell Sherbert, a Seventh-day Adventist, had been fired from a mill because she would not work on Saturdays due to her church's teachings. Unable to find another job, Sherbert applied for unemployment compensation but was denied. The state's Employment Security Commission deemed her refusal to work on Saturdays a disqualification for receiving benefits.

Writing for the Court, Justice Brennan held that the denial of unemployment benefits violated the free exercise clause. He commanded a majority that held that "indirect" burdens, whether intentional or not, no less than "direct" burdens on religious minorities, are actionable under the First Amendment. Sherbert faced a "cruel choice" in adhering to her faith but forfeiting the benefits. He also found it significant that South Carolina did not deny benefits to those who worshipped on Sundays; thus the state was not neutral with respect to all religions.

Significantly, Justice Brennan laid down a two-pronged test for judging such claims. When a law, although neutral toward religion, burdens religious minorities, the government must demonstrate (1) a "compelling state interest" in its regulation and (2) that it cannot advance its interests by the "least restrictive means." On that basis, he rejected South Carolina's argument that the denial of benefits advanced its interests in preventing fraudulent claims and in safeguarding its unemployment compensation fund. Those interests could be advanced by other less drastic means without burdening Sherbert's religious freedom. Like *Cantwell*, the ruling in *Sherbert* came to be considered another landmark in the First Amendment's expanding protection for religious minorities.

———

The direction of the Warren Court's rulings angered conservatives. The Court was denounced for eroding federalism and for taking prayer out of the public schools. In 1968, as part of his strategy to win over southern white Democratic voters, Republican presidential candidate Richard M. Nixon promised to appoint justices who were opposed to the "judicial activism" of the Warren Court and who were "strict constructionists."

Nixon won the election and subsequently named four justices. In 1969, he appointed Chief Justice Warren E. Burger, a conservative on the Court of Appeals for the District of Columbia Circuit. The following year, after controversies forced the withdrawal of two other nominees, he elevated another federal appellate court judge, Harry A. Blackmun. In 1972, he named his last two appointees: Lewis F. Powell, a former president of the American Bar Association, and William H. Rehnquist, a young conservative assistant attorney general in the Department of Justice.

The Burger Court gradually moved in a more conservative direction, particularly on the rights of accused criminals. Chief Justice Burger disagreed with many of the Warren Court's precedents. In particular, he deemed that its rulings on the separation of religion from the state demonstrated hostility toward religion. In *Lemon v. Kurtzman* (1971), he commanded a majority in adopting a new three-pronged test for applying the (dis)establishment clause: whether a law (1) has a secular purpose (2) whose primary effect is neither to advance nor inhibit religion and (3) does not foster "an excessive government entanglement with religion." The *Lemon* test was formulated to permit greater governmental accommodation of religion, but it proved to be no sure guide. It was applied in seemingly conflicting ways and was sometimes simply ignored.

Unlike conservatives who were dismissive of free exercise claims, however, Chief Justice Burger thought that the Court should accommodate religious minorities when generally applicable laws impose burdens, at least in the absence of a compelling governmental interest. The Burger Court thus continued to apply *Sherbert* to prohibit the denial of unemployment benefits to a Jehovah's Witness who refused to work in a steel mill that produced military weapons in *Thomas v. Review Board of Indiana* (1981). *Sherbert* and that decision was then reaffirmed in *Hobbie v. Unemployment Appeals Commission of Florida* (1987) and later in *Frazee v. Illinois Department of Employment Security* (1989).

The Burger Court's major ruling on the free exercise clause came in *Wisconsin v. Yoder* (1972), in which Amish parents challenged a compulsory school attendance law. The Warren Court had upheld a similar law in *Garber v. Kansas* (1967), but the Court in *Yoder* ruled that states may not compel Amish children to attend school up to the age of sixteen.

Jonas Yoder, Wallace Miller, and Adin Yutzy were convicted of violating Wisconsin's compulsory school attendance law, which required all children to attend school until age sixteen. Yoder, Miller, and Yutzy refused to send their children, ages fourteen and fifteen, to public school after the eighth grade. They contended that an eighth-grade education was all their children needed to live within the Amish community, and the law infringed on their free exercise of religion. A state appeals court disagreed, but Wisconsin's state supreme court reversed.

Chief Justice Burger affirmed the state supreme court and advanced an accommodationist approach to the First Amendment's protection for religious minorities. To be sure, he narrowly tailored his opinion by emphasizing the unique religious traditions of the Amish, to discourage other religious minorities from seeking exemptions from otherwise generally applicable laws. Nonetheless, citing *Sherbert*, he stressed that governmental interests deemed sufficient to override free exercise claims in prior cases "invariably posed some substantial threat to public safety, peace or order," which was not the case here. In his view, "only those [governmental] interests of the highest order and those not otherwise served can over balance legitimate claims to the free exercise of religion."

Wisconsin v. Yoder invited religious minorities to bring litigation challenging other generally applicable laws, and the Burger Court generally held the line. *United States v. Lee* (1982), for instance, held that Amish employers must pay Social Security taxes for their employees, even though Congress exempted self-employed Amish from paying the tax. The Court also upheld the Internal Revenue Service's withdrawal of the tax-exempt status of a Christian university that preached racial discrimination in *Bob Jones University and Goldsboro Christian School v. United States* (1983). It ruled that religious organizations must comply with federal minimum-wage laws in *Tony and Susan Alamo Foundation v. Secretary of Labor* (1985) and upheld the government's use of Social Security numbers over religious objections in *Bowen v. Roy* (1986). In *Goldman v. Weinberger* (1986), a bare majority upheld the air force's prohibition on the wearing of yarmulkes by Orthodox Jewish officers. In all these cases, the government was found to have a compelling interest overriding the claims for religious exemption.

The Burger Court, though, also upheld the claim of a Jehovah's Witness, George Maynard, who objected to being compelled to bear the New Hampshire state motto "Live Free or Die" on his license plates. New Hampshire's attorney general at the time, David Hackett Souter (subsequently named to the federal appellate bench and then to the high court in 1990 by George H.W. Bush), defended the law. He argued that it advanced the state's interest in helping police officers distinguish passenger cars from commercial vehicles, whose plates did not bear the motto. But in *Wooley v. Maynard* (1977), Chief Justice Burger rejected that justification as not compelling. The state could advance its interests in a less restrictive way without denying Maynard's religious freedom. Likewise, the Burger Court unanimously held that religious leaders may not be disqualified from serving as delegates to a state constitutional convention in *McDaniel v. Paty* (1978). To hold otherwise would violate the principle of religious neutrality and nondiscrimination.

The Rehnquist Court Turns Course

By the 1980s, the Burger Court was a profound disappointment to conservatives. The political landscape had shifted farther and faster to the right than the Court, and Chief Justice Burger appeared to lack the intellectual wherewithal to lead it. Justice Blackmun authored the abortion ruling in *Roe v. Wade* and increasingly voted with liberals. Justice Powell was a swing voter in major controversies and was inclined to abide by liberal precedents. Republican President Gerald R. Ford's appointment of Justice John Paul Stevens in 1975 was no less disappointing. Stevens was a maverick and unpredictable. Only Justice Rehnquist championed a solidly conservative line, writing more solo dissents than any other justice, which earned him the nickname the "Lone Ranger."

The Burger Court both failed to forge a "constitutional counter-revolution" and upheld abortion, court-ordered busing to achieve integration, and most affirmative action programs, as well as gave greater scope to the Fourteenth Amendment's equal protection clause. Those rulings, no less than the Warren Court, embittered the New Christian Right, "movement conservatives," and others in the coalition behind the election of Republican President Ronald Reagan.

Reagan vowed to appoint justices who were opposed to past "judicial activism" and respected the "original intent" of the framers of the Constitution. In his 1980 presidential campaign, he also promised to appoint the first woman to the Supreme Court. In 1981, he named Justice Sandra Day O'Connor, a conservative Republican judge on an Arizona state appellate court. Then in 1987 he made a major mark by elevating Rehnquist to chief justice and filling his seat with Antonin Scalia, a former University of Chicago Law School professor who is a champion of a jurisprudence of original intent. The next year, Justice Powell stepped down, and Reagan's nomination of Judge Robert H. Bork — a former solicitor general and professor at Yale Law School — became ensnarled in a bitter confirmation battle. Bork was eventually defeated in the Senate. Reagan finally filled the seat in 1988 with Anthony Kennedy, a more moderate, less doctrinaire conservative judge from the Court of Appeals for the Ninth Circuit.

The Rehnquist Court soon moved in a sharply more conservative direction. The divisions among the justices over religious freedom became more pronounced as well. The most conservative justices — Rehnquist and Scalia — embraced the nonpreferentialist approach to the (dis)establishment clause and vigorously sought to lower the "high wall" of separation between the state and religion. They also strongly opposed excepting religious minorities from generally applicable laws. By contrast, the liberal justices — Brennan, Marshall, Stevens, and Blackmun — took diametrically opposite positions on the religion clauses. They stood by the "high wall" theory in interpreting the (dis)establishment clause and defended claims of religious freedom under the free exercise clause. Justices O'Connor and Kennedy, the centrists, generally embraced an accommodationist approach toward cases involving governmental aid to religion and to free exercise claims in the absence of compelling, overriding governmental interests. In particular, Kennedy proved to be a vigorous defender of the principle of religious nondiscrimination because of his reading of the intersection of the First Amendment's guarantees and the Fourteenth Amendment's equal protection clause.

In the late 1980s, the Rehnquist Court signaled that it looked less favorably on claims of religious minorities than the Warren and Burger Courts had. *Lyng v. Northwest Indian Cemetery Protective Association* (1988), for example, upheld the Forest Service's allowance of timber harvesting in areas of national parks that were traditionally set aside for religious use by Indian tribes. In *Hernandez v. Commissioner of Internal Revenue* (1989), a majority of the Rehnquist Court held that certain donations to the Church of Scientology were not tax deductible. California's sales tax as applied to religious materials sold at evangelical crusades and by mail order was also upheld in *Jimmy Swaggart Ministries v. Board of Equalization of California* (1990).

The Rehnquist Court's first major pronouncement on the free exercise clause came in *Employment Division, Department of Human Resources of Oregon v. Smith* (1990), a case involving the denial of unemployment compensation. In *Oregon v. Smith*, Justice Scalia abandoned *Sherbert v. Verner*'s analysis. He held that indirect burdens on religious minorities, such as the denial of unemployment benefits, that resulted from their violation of otherwise generally applicable laws do not violate the First Amendment. Justice O'Connor concurred but sharply disagreed with the abandonment of *Sherbert*. Justices Brennan and Marshall joined Justice Blackmun's bitter dissent.

Oregon v. Smith stemmed from the firing of Alfred Smith and Galen Black from their jobs as drug rehabilitation counselors because they took peyote (an intoxicating drug produced from mescal cacti). Both men were members of the Native American Church and ingested peyote only for sacramental purposes. When they applied for unemployment compensation, Oregon's Employment Division denied them benefits on the grounds that they had been discharged for work-related misconduct. They challenged the denial of unemployment benefits and sued, relying on *Sherbert v. Verner.* A state appellate court agreed with them, and after the state appealed, the Oregon Supreme Court affirmed the lower court. The state supreme court construed the purpose of the misconduct provision as being to preserve the financial integrity of the state's compensation fund, not to enforce the state's criminal laws against drug usage. Citing *Sherbert*, the Oregon Supreme Court concluded that Smith and Black were entitled to unemployment benefits because the state's interest in a solvent compensation fund did not outweigh the burden imposed on the men's religious beliefs.

In 1987, Oregon appealed that decision to the Supreme Court. It contended that its criminal laws against peyote consumption were relevant to balancing the state's interest in denying benefits against the men's First Amendment claims. In *Employment Division, Department of Human Resources of Oregon v. Smith (Smith I)*, a majority of the justices agreed with the state and vacated the decision. In remanding the case, the Court noted that the state supreme court had not decided whether the sacramental use of peyote was proscribed under state law. Until the state court ruled on that issue, the Court declined to address the First Amendment claim or the merits of the case. On remand, the Oregon Supreme Court held that its state law, unlike those elsewhere, made no exception for the sacramental use of peyote; nevertheless, it reaffirmed its previous holding. Oregon again appealed to the Supreme Court.

Writing for the Court in *Oregon v. Smith (Smith II)*, Justice Scalia distinguished prior rulings following *Sherbert v. Verner* that did not involve conduct prohibited by law — in this case, peyote use. Although he reaffirmed that the First Amendment forbids "governmental regulation of religious *beliefs* as such," citing *Sherbert*, he ruled that a religious practice that runs afoul of neutral and generally applicable criminal laws does not merit an exception or justify judicial protection under the free exercise clause. Notably, he specifically cited Judge Spellman's decision upholding Hialeah's prohibition of ritual animal sacrifice as another neutral and generally applicable criminal law.

Justice Scalia proceeded to reject *Sherbert*'s analysis. His bottom line was striking and remains in sharp contrast to Justice Jackson's ringing defense of First Amendment freedoms in *West Virginia State Board of Education v. Barnette*. Justice Scalia boldly proclaimed:

> To say that a nondiscriminatory religious-practice exemption is permitted, or even that it is desirable, is not to say that it is constitutionally required, and that the appropriate occasions for its creation can be discerned by the courts. It may fairly be said that leaving accommodation to the political process will place at a relative disadvantage those religious practices that are not widely engaged in; but that unavoidable consequence of democratic government must be preferred to a system in which each conscience is a law unto itself or in which judges weigh the social importance of all laws against the centrality of all religious beliefs.

Obviously troubled by Justice Scalia's analysis, language, and rejection of *Sherbert*, concurring Justice O'Connor strenuously objected to the majority's dismissive approach to the free exercise clause. "In my view," she said, "today's holding dramatically departs from well-settled First Amendment jurisprudence, appears unnecessary to resolve the question presented, and is incompatible with our Nation's fundamental commitment to individual religious liberty." Justice O'Connor also expressly doubted that any state or locality would enact laws specifically targeting particular religions or religious practices.

Dissenting Justice Blackmun was even more impassioned in challenging Justice Scalia's opinion for "mischaracterizing this Court's precedents," discarding "leading free exercise cases such as *Cantwell v. Connecticut* (1940) and *Wisconsin v. Yoder* (1972)," and abandoning *Sherbert v. Verner*. "This Court," he reminded his colleagues, "has developed a consistent and exacting standard to test the constitutionality of a state statute that burdens the free exercise of religion. Such a statute may stand only if the law in general, and the State's refusal to allow a religious exemption in particular, are justified by a compelling interest that cannot be served by less restrictive means."

Justice Scalia's ruling and opinion in *Oregon v. Smith* provoked a major controversy outside the Court as well. Virtually every major religious organization disagreed with it and protested the abandonment of *Sherbert v. Verner*. After almost three decades, *Sherbert* had become a landmark in the protection of religious minorities. A broad coalition of religious organizations and interest groups lobbied Congress to enact legislation overriding *Oregon v. Smith* and restoring *Sherbert*'s test for protecting religious minorities. Attorneys affiliated with a number of those organizations also set out to find a case that might be appealed to the Court and serve as a vehicle for persuading the justices to reconsider and overrule *Smith*.

———

As with most cases that reach the Supreme Court, precedents and doctrines provided a basis for good arguments on both sides of *Church of the Lukumi v. City of Hialeah*, though in light of the ruling in *Oregon v. Smith*, the direction of the Rehnquist Court did not appear to bode well for Pichardo and his church.

Attorneys for the church could argue that Hialeah had targeted a particular religion, thereby violating the principle of religious neutrality and nondiscrimination. The ordinances directly burdened the beliefs and practices of followers of Santeria, and the ban against ritual animal sacrifice was not a neutral and generally applicable criminal law. It singled out *ritual* animal sacrifices, obviously targeting a particular religious practice. The city did not ban hunting, fishing, or other kinds of killing of animals. Hialeah had no compelling governmental interest, nor had the city shown that it could not advance its interests in health, safety, and welfare by less drastic means. Even under *Oregon v. Smith*, Hialeah could not directly burden religion. *Smith* applied only to claims of indirect burdens on religious freedom, not to overt religious discrimination by the government.

Garrett could argue contrariwise. He could defend the ordinances as merely regulating conduct, like polygamy. Hialeah was not suppressing or censoring beliefs in Santeria. The ordinances were generally applicable laws and did not target a particular religion. Pagans, Satanists, and others — not just followers of Santeria — were barred from ritual animal sacrifices. The city also had a compelling interest in banning ritual animal sacrifice. The large number of discarded animal carcasses posed risks to public health and safety, and the city had an interest in preventing animal cruelty. Finally, the ordinances were a proper exercise of the city's police powers, just like criminalizing the use of peyote and other drugs.

CHAPTER 4

Rituals on Trial

At the outset, the assignment of Ernesto Pichardo's case to Judge Eugene P. Spellman appeared to bode well. Although a year earlier he had found no basis for holding Hialeah's mayor and city council liable under Section 1983 for harassing and violating the constitutional rights of Pichardo and other church members, Spellman had a reputation as a liberal-oriented jurist who took the Constitution seriously. Even Pichardo thought: "If there was any judge who could understand what was going on, he was the one."

Judge Spellman was born in New York City in 1930 but grew up in Miami. He graduated from Miami Senior High School and received his undergraduate and law degrees from the University of Florida in Gainesville. After graduating, he worked as a law clerk for a state appellate court. He then served as an assistant state attorney general for criminal appeals in Tallahassee, before becoming an assistant state attorney for Dade County, heading its Rackets and Frauds Division. For almost two decades, from 1961 to 1979, he was in private practice. By all accounts, he was devoted to community service, serving on the boards of various civic organizations.

Judge Spellman, a Catholic Democrat, was appointed to the federal bench in 1979 by Democratic President Jimmy Carter. Early in his judicial career, he earned a reputation as a rather courageous judge — "the little giant," as he was known in the local Haitian community. In 1980–1981, faced with the influx of Cubans from the Mariel boatlift and potentially another 50,000 Haitian exiles, the Reagan administration decided to get tough — interdicting boats on the high seas and putting any undocumented Haitians found aboard in detention camps in Florida and Arkansas. In doing so, it revived a policy abandoned in 1954 with the closing of Ellis Island in New York, where most immigrants had arrived. Some Haitian refugees detained by the Immigration and Naturalization Service (INS) challenged the constitutionality of the new detention policy, arguing that it was unlawful and discriminatory. The INS countered that it was neither. Haitians, unlike Cubans, were not seeking political asylum; they were only escaping the poverty of their island.

In the case of the Haitian refugees, Judge Spellman ruled that the detention policy was illegal. The INS had failed to give notice of the policy change in the *Federal Register*. He also decried the tactics of the INS and found that Haitians were being treated discriminatorily and denied due process. Consequently, Judge Spellman faced considerable local opposition. Attorneys for the Justice Department and the INS argued that an estimated 50,000 Haitians would leave their temporary haven in the Bahamas for South Florida if he ordered the release of some 1,900 Haitians then detained in camps. He concluded, however, that there was "no evidence establishing that fact" and ordered the parole of detainees to local community organizations. The Court of Appeals for the Eleventh Circuit subsequently upheld his decision.

A Judge Embattled

Judge Spellman heard arguments in the case over nine days, usually three to four hours each day. The trial began on July 31 and continued throughout August, with closing arguments on August 28, 1989. From one perspective, the trial was unremarkable, though admittedly its focus on the First Amendment's protection of ritual animal sacrifice was unusual.

Trials begin with pretrial hearings and opening arguments, followed by the introduction of evidence, testimony and cross-examination of witnesses, and then closing arguments. At pretrial hearings, lawyers file motions for discovery and to exclude evidence, and judges must decide what to admit or reject. In effect, pretrial hearings are studied attempts to choreograph what happens during the trial — what competing narratives will be told and who will tell them. During the trial, judges hear competing stories offered by counsel about what the law is or should be and what the facts are. Witnesses testify and are cross-examined to underscore their persuasiveness or, alternatively, undermine their credibility. There are plenty of opportunities to distort, contradict, and discredit the testimony and the evidence presented.

That is the heart of the adversary system. It is based on what Judge Jerome Frank called "the fight theory" in his classic work *Courts on Trial*. Trials aim at fairness, not at ascertaining the truth, certainly not the truth in any scientific sense. Trials aim at the truth only as it is socially reconstructed and contested in accordance with procedural rules and as played out in each trial. Attorneys are supposed to battle it out in front of an impartial judge. However, the very premises and processes of the adversarial system, as former federal court judge Marvin Frankel observed, may "embattle" judges as well.

What began rather routinely during the course of the pretrial hearings and later the trial appeared to try the patience of, if not embattle, Judge Spellman. Both sides attempted to block the discovery process, and Garrett recalled that the level of frustration ran very high. Judge Spellman also formed his first, and perhaps lasting, impressions of the personalities involved. At one point, for instance, he ordered Pichardo to turn over the church's membership list. Pichardo and Duarte refused, vigorously objecting that it was protected by the First Amendment's guarantee of freedom of association. Judge Spellman ultimately reconsidered and did not find Pichardo in contempt of court, but a heated confrontation with Duarte and a disrespectful gesture he made in the courtroom led Spellman to fine him for his behavior. That and other incidents, as Garrett observed, "telegraphed" messages to the judge about the personalities he was dealing with, and that became evident in his final ruling.

On the opening day of the trial, the courtroom was crowded with the mayor's supporters and animal rights advocates on one side and Pichardo and the church's supporters on the other. Lawyers for both sides made their opening statements outlining their basic arguments.

In his opening statement, Duarte argued that Hialeah's ordinances were unconstitutional. Although his statement was somewhat rambling, he made the key points. Hialeah had targeted a particular religion in violation of the First Amendment's free exercise clause. "Santeria is an established religion with origins in Nigeria," he explained, "and animal sacrifice is an integral part of the religion." The city's ordinances were part of a continuing "pattern of harassment."

Even if the ordinances were upheld, he contended, animal sacrifice as practiced by the *santeros* should be exempt from regulation for the same reason Jewish ritual slaughter was exempt. The church, he concluded, sought an injunction to prevent Hialeah from enforcing its ordinances. Horwich, who represented both Pichardo and the church, briefly reviewed the First Amendment claims. Rosen, appearing on behalf of Pichardo, briefly pressed the Section 1983 claim for liability if the ordinances were found to run afoul of constitutional rights.

Garrett likewise summarized his main points. The ordinances did not target religion; they were neither discriminatory nor a harassment of religion. Instead, they had been passed during an election year at the urging of many of Hialeah's most prominent religious leaders. They were simply an attempt to regulate the killing of animals and the disposal of their remains. The ordinances advanced the city's interests, first, by protecting the health, safety, and welfare of its residents; discarded animal carcasses in public places posed health risks. Second, Hialeah had an interest in preventing cruelty to animals; ritualized sacrifice caused animals unnecessary fear, pain, and suffering, and it was obviously cruel. Third, the city had an interest in protecting the welfare of children, and ritual animal sacrifice posed particular dangers for children witnessing the rites. "It could cause them to be more violent," Garrett claimed. For these reasons, Hialeah's ordinances should be upheld.

After the opening arguments, the witnesses against and for the city testified and were cross-examined, and what had begun rather routinely quickly became convoluted and at times bizarre. The twists and turns were even more unexpected because the two sides were so mismatched in terms of their resources. This is often the case in disputes between religious minorities and governmental authorities.

In Judge Spellman's courtroom, the two sides were definitely not on the adversarial system's theoretically even playing field. The church had virtually no resources, and the ACLU's financial support paid for only basic costs. There was no money to pay for high-powered expert witnesses, so Duarte had to call local community college teachers and psychological experts in support of his side. By contrast, Garrett and Hialeah had state and local officials on their side. Michael Neiman of the state attorney general's office filed a brief in support of the ordinances and appeared as counsel. Garrett could also afford to pay for prominent legal and medical experts to be flown down to Miami to testify.

In spite of the mismatch of resources, it seems fair to say that no one's testimony counted for more than Pichardo's. As the outspoken priest most closely identified with the church and a named plaintiff in the suit, he was at center stage. But for Judge Spellman, Pichardo's testimony proved to be at times bewildering and — whether sincere or not — ultimately unbelievable.

Arguing the Church's Case

Ernesto Pichardo is serious, committed, and provocative. He is as tenacious as any other religious minority willing to fight for his faith all the way to the Supreme Court. He is foxy and clever but can also be brash and combative. All these traits came into play during his testimony.

Pichardo testified about virtually every aspect of the Church of the Lukumi and Santeria. Much of it Judge Spellman found puzzling and possibly disingenuous. Pichardo testified, for example, that the church's primary goal was education, not performing ritual animal sacrifices. The case, though, was about the city's banning of ritual animal sacrifices, not research and education in religion. By "establishing and promoting research among scholars to research this faith," he testified, "we can in fact educate right across the board, our religious community and those who are not our religious community."

Moreover, Pichardo explained, when the church moved from its original location at 173 West Fifth Street in December 1987 to a yellow storefront at 700 Palm Avenue, on Hialeah's main shopping street and almost directly across from city hall, it was understood that zoning regulations prohibited animal sacrifices. "We knew that 700 Palm Avenue is not zoned for any animal sacrifices and we never intended to have it at that location." At its new location, the church's mission was strictly educational; its focus was on educating the non-Santeria public, not followers of the religion.

Pichardo nonetheless appeared to contradict that testimony by revealing that two weeks before the trial began, the church had applied for a license to operate as a slaughterhouse, because city employees had allegedly told him that animal sacrifices could then be performed there.

He also claimed that due to Hialeah's ordinances banning animal sacrifice, "in the meantime, we're handcuffed." The city had effectively barred them from performing that religious ritual. He further argued that Santeria would become more understood if the Church of the Lukumi were allowed to practice its rituals openly. The church might "absorb the thousands that are out there in South Florida and have them come in and not hide behind closed doors because of fear of persecution and discrimination and what have you."

At the same time, though, he had no idea how many followers of Santeria might actually join the church. At one point, he denied having any certain knowledge of how Santeria was practiced in Hialeah or how many followers there were, since he had devoted himself to research and education.

It became evident to Judge Spellman that Pichardo and the church were not exactly in sync with the traditions and practices of the broader Santeria community in South Florida. On the one hand, Pichardo agreed that Santeria was based on oral traditions, and traditionally there had been no organized or centralized authority. Santeria, he testified, "does not have this center where people can go and you can monitor and you have a number of controls over that religious community." On the other hand, Pichardo submitted as an exhibit his Code of Beliefs and Code of Ethics, which he had prepared for the church. He testified that they correctly set forth the oral traditions he had been taught, and he sought to assure Judge Spellman that they were authentic, true to the religious tradition of worshipping the *orishas*. In addition, he emphasized that the church had established its own internal identification techniques for priests, including a "fining system" for "deviants" and "testing" procedures to determine "true" followers.

Pichardo claimed that the Church of the Lukumi was turning an oral tradition into a written one and that it would institutionalize and open to the public a religion that historically had not been hierarchical and traditionally had been practiced in secret. These claims struck Judge Spellman as incredible. As he would explain: "Pichardo gave no evidence to support his claim [of the authenticity of his 'codes'], and in fact has consistently testified that he doesn't even know which members of the Church are priests." He found Pichardo's testimony less than forthcoming at best, if not disingenuous.

Consequently, in his opinion, Judge Spellman made much of the fact that Pichardo had testified that he held the second highest priesthood rank of an *oba* or *italero* but did not know the number of Santeria practitioners in Hialeah, how many were priests, or what ranks they held. Judge Spellman found it inconceivable that Pichardo could claim that there were about ten *italeros* in Miami-Dade County but that he knew only two. Pichardo acknowledged that an annual conference of Cuban and Puerto Rican Santeria priests was held in New York, but he had neither been invited nor ever attended one. To Judge Spellman, Santeria was not a mainstream religion, and Pichardo and his church appeared to be on the fringe of the larger Santeria community.

Clearly not amused, Judge Spellman showed his impatience with Pichardo and Duarte throughout the trial. At a pointed moment during Pichardo's testimony about the church and its plans, for instance, he interrupted to ask: "Would I be less than candid in saying that this is more right now in your mind a dream than it is a reality?"

"No," responded Pichardo. "I would not say that would be fair." He felt that Judge Spellman viewed "him as a foreign object intruding on American society. Spellman was true to his last name. He sat there in a spell. I was an alien to this man."

Pichardo also testified at length about the Santeria practice of sacrificing animals — chickens, pigeons, doves, ducks, guinea pigs, goats, sheep, and turtles. That testimony apparently struck Judge Spellman as just as fanciful or incomprehensible as Pichardo's testimony about the Santeria priesthood.

Pichardo testified that only priests or priestesses perform animal sacrifices, and they do so according to their training. Most of the animals are consumed after the rituals, unless they are used in healing rites; in those rites, the illness or sickness passes from the client to the animal. However, he also claimed that the priests were not involved in "the obtaining, maintaining, butchering, cooking or disposing of the sacrificial animals." Judge Spellman found it revealing that, although he was a high priest, Pichardo claimed to be "unaware of how those other functions were actually performed, although he did state that the animals were expected to be healthy, clean and free of disease."

Furthermore, Pichardo testified that priests receive no training in how to tell whether an animal is healthy and rely only on their own observations. He also said that he had never disposed of an animal carcass and did not know what was actually done with the remains of the sacrificed animals. According to him, different priests were trained to perform different functions. Some obtained and inspected the animals, others sacrificed them, and still others cooked them and cleaned up. All this appeared bewildering, if not unbelievable, to Judge Spellman.

As for how animals are sacrificed, Pichardo testified that the ritual is learned through initiation and apprenticeship with a senior priest. The animal is placed on a table on its left side, with the apprentice holding the hind legs. Standing behind the animal and table, the priest holds the head so it faces away and extends over the edge of the table, above clay pots into which its blood will drip. Holding a knife in the right hand, the priest severs the main arteries of the neck in one quick movement. This practice, he claimed, was generally reliable and painless. However, experts who testified for Hialeah disputed that, and Judge Spellman would ultimately conclude that they were more credible.

After the animal is sacrificed, Pichardo testified, the blood drains into the clay pots. The animal is then decapitated and removed. Although he claimed that the blood is removed and disposed of, how this is accomplished remained another "mystery" for Judge Spellman. Accordingly, Judge Spellman found more "credible testimony that the blood is at times actually drunk, placed on individuals, or left in pots for long periods." Although Pichardo countered that such practices are deviant, many other practitioners of and authorities on Santeria endorsed such uses of animal blood as traditional practice.

Much was also made about the sacrifice of animals during initiation rites. Such rites last for seven nights, with the initiate confined in a sacred room for the entire week. On the second night, between twenty and thirty animals are sacrificed — usually six four-legged animals and twenty-four chickens, depending on which and how many *orishas* are involved in the rite. Given the large number of animals sacrificed during initiation rites, the matter of disposing of the carcasses again loomed large. That ostensibly remained the major and central problem facing the city. But in response to questioning, Pichardo testified that the church would comply with any legal requirements for the disposal of animal carcasses — whether that involved their burial, incineration, or disposal in sanitary waste containers.

Still, that testimony struck Judge Spellman as untenable. Pichardo had testified that there was no way for the city — or, for that matter, the court — to address how practitioners of Santeria who did not belong to his church disposed of animal carcasses. Judge Spellman later made much of this in his opinion, apparently because he had concluded that Pichardo's claims were unrealistic.

Judge Spellman focused attention as well on the practice of divination. Divination is used to determine the type of animal to be sacrificed, based on the purpose of performing the sacrifice. Divination also determines how the animal's remains are to be disposed of. Priests perform divination based on the *Ifa* cycle of 256 *odus* (principles), each of which is further subdivided into groups of sixteen. They are represented by different combinations of black and white marks on cowrie shells and, by some *santeros*, on the inside of coconut rinds. The priest casts them and reads their pattern, thereby communicating with the *orishas*.

Certainly, in light of testimony about the practice of divination, Judge Spellman was unpersuaded by Pichardo's testimony that the church would comply with any regulations on the disposal of animal carcasses, even though some *santeros* might conclude that divination ordered the disposal of carcasses in public places — below special palm trees, on beaches, or at crossroads — depending on why the animal was sacrificed. According to Pichardo, the church considered such interpretations of the disposal of carcasses to be "deviant," a departure from the authentic religious practice, yet he conceded that many *santeros* disagreed.

Judge Spellman was left incredulous. How could Pichardo testify that such interpretations of divination were deviant yet maintain that *santeros* outside the church might plausibly claim otherwise. As Judge Spellman put it: "Pichardo could give this Court no assurance that those who follow, in his eyes, a deviant form of Santeria, would conform to any regulations at all. Additionally, the religion has always been a secret religion and much is still not known."

"It is inconceivable," Judge Spellman concluded, "that the religious practitioners would accept the type of regulatory controls on their activities that such conformity would require, especially in light of the fact that their sacrifices, by the terms of their religion, must be kept secret and cannot be monitored. A less restrictive ordinance simply could not be enforced."

Defending Hialeah's Ordinances

Although the church was outgunned by the high-powered expert witnesses called by Garrett, some of them proved to be less than helpful, if not counterproductive. For instance, Marc Paulhus, director of the southeast regional office of the Humane Society in Tallahassee and an active supporter of Hialeah's ordinances, testified about cruelty to animals but also reached beyond his expertise. He claimed, for example, that Voodoo and Santeria were both religions blending elements of African religion and Christianity. Yet he had also called Santeria "a bloody cult . . . whose continued presence further blights the image of South Florida."

A deputy city attorney testified that the Church of the Lukumi was not a slaughterhouse. But virtually everyone on both sides of the controversy knew that the church's attempt to obtain a license to operate as a slaughterhouse was merely a subterfuge.

More persuasive for Judge Spellman in concluding that Pichardo and the church did not represent all practitioners of Santeria was the testimony of Dr. Lisandro Perez, a sociologist and professor at Florida International University. Perez, who had immigrated from Cuba in the 1960s at age eleven, strongly disagreed with Pichardo that Santeria would become more open if the church were allowed to conduct ritual animal sacrifices openly. "There may be a lot of *santeros*," as he put it, "who may not wish to place their beliefs on a public sort of marketplace." If the outcome of the case favored the church, it would almost certainly not end the practice of ritual animal sacrifice in private homes.

The leading and most impressive expert witness for Judge Spellman was Dr. Michael Fox. A veterinarian and the author of more than thirty books, Fox received his degree from the Royal Veterinary College in London, along with a Ph.D. in medicine from the University of London. At the time, he was the vice president of the Humane Society of the United States in Washington, D.C. In the 1980s, he played a major role in moving the HSUS beyond traditional concerns about animal welfare to more aggressive advocacy of animal rights.

Fox sharply disputed testimony that Santeria's method of sacrificing animals is humane and painless. According to him, it is patently inhumane. There is no way of guaranteeing that the person performing the sacrifice will cut through both carotid arteries at the same time. Furthermore, the lining of one artery might recoil and close, thereby preventing instant hemorrhaging and death. In addition, Fox pointed out that animals differ in their arterial makeup. Young goats and sheep, for example, have deep arteries. Unless their necks are completely severed, there is no assurance that they will be rendered instantly unconscious. If all the arteries are not severed simultaneously, they become unconscious "slowly," over a period of "many seconds to minutes."

Especially problematic is the sacrifice of chickens. For one thing, chickens have four carotid arteries — two internal and two external. Their arteries are very rubbery and tend to slide. Consequently, when chickens are sacrificed, the possibility of missing one or more of the arteries increases. Chickens are therefore highly unlikely to die instantly or painlessly.

Fox's testimony about the suffering of animals sacrificed according to the traditions of Santeria was not unproblematic, however. By his standard, the Santeria practice was inhumane because there was no guarantee the animals would die instantly. But if that standard were applied uniformly, kosher slaughterhouses might be outlawed or more stringently regulated. Fox conceded that the Jewish and Muslim knife strokes from the front of an animal's throat might be more reliable than the stroke of a *santero*'s knife from behind, cutting from one side to the other. Still, under cross-examination he maintained that animals butchered in kosher slaughterhouses frequently do not die immediately. For that reason, he supported more restrictive regulations on Jewish and Muslim slaughterhouses as well.

The prospect of sacrificed animals dying in fear and pain was also highly likely, Fox testified, because prior to Santeria rites, animals are usually kept in close confinement with other animals — in *botanicas*, for instance. Close confinement with other species undoubtedly caused stress and anxiety, which would be compounded if the animals were sacrificed in places where others had just been sacrificed, such as during an initiation rite. The animals would smell the bodily secretions and odors of the other animals, triggering an intense reaction of fear. That fear might not always be noticeable, however, because the animals could develop "tonic immobility," freezing out of fear.

Turning again to the sacrifice of chickens, Fox emphasized that the stress and trauma experienced by them was particularly dangerous for humans. Under stress, the chickens' immune systems increase the production of salmonella bacteria, which can infect people and cannot be detected by simple observation.

In response to Fox's testimony, Duarte called a local pathologist, Dr. Charles Wetli. During the previous decade as deputy chief medical examiner for Dade County, he had frequently been called to inspect skeletal remains. As a result, he became interested in Santeria and came to appreciate the religious beliefs associated with its practices. Ritual animal sacrifice did not trouble him. Indeed, at the time, he had just contributed a foreword and several photographs for Migene Gonzalez-Wippler's 1989 book *Santeria: The Religion*.

Wetli contradicted Fox's testimony. The Santeria method of sacrificing animals, in his view, resulted in rapid death. Based on his experience, the animals were killed in a humane fashion. He admitted, though, that an animal's interpretation of pain might not be the same as that of a human.

Judge Spellman dismissed Wetli's testimony almost completely out of hand. Wetli, he explained, "was not a veterinarian and has no knowledge of any biological differences that might impact on his evaluation." He therefore found "that the testimony of Dr. Fox, with his specialized knowledge, is more credible in this area." He was persuaded by Fox's "conclusions that the method used in sacrificing the animals is not humane, but in fact causes fear and pain to the animal."

More problematic for Garrett was another witness he called in support of the city's interests in promoting health, safety, and welfare by reducing the risk of disease from discarded carcasses. The testimony of Walter R. Livingstone, the environmental administrator for the Dade County Department of Public Health, proved to be a mixed blessing. Livingstone testified that the health dangers from dead animals arose from many sources, not primarily from *santeros* discarding carcasses. In Livingstone's words: "We do find dead chickens or dead animals, dead fish is one thing, dead garbage in fact, garbage from restaurants and things like that, animal meat parts and things like that this is where they provide the food for the rat, the rat comes and then seeks a harborage area and makes regular runs."

Notably, Duarte asked whether restaurants were "probably the largest place that rats congregate?" Livingstone replied: "I wouldn't say the largest. They're very commonplace. Because of the very fact that we have so many other facilities. A lot of times, public buildings are a good place. Restaurants would be one because, generally speaking, because of the garbage, they provide a lot of food for the rodents."

Surprisingly and unwittingly undercutting Garrett's defense of the ordinances, Livingstone added: "I don't believe what we're talking about here today has anything to do with animal sacrifice. It is just the way that food, chickens, parts, et cetera, are handled and their presence can increase the spread of disease. As I said before, you are trying to change this into animal sacrifice, and I haven't been speaking of animal sacrifice at all. I am talking about the possibility, the probability, the transmission of disease from animal to human via the desecration, via the situations you have asked me about all day."

As if that were not damaging enough, Livingstone further testified that the Dade County Department of Public Health received "frequent complaints from neighbors about the way that veterinarians dispose of their animal remains." Under questioning, he agreed that the problem of properly disposing of animal carcasses could be addressed in other less drastic ways. It was safe, for instance, to simply put carcasses in plastic bags and then put them into garbage cans.

No less troubling for Garrett's defense of Hialeah's ordinances was the testimony of the director of animal services for Dade County, Zorida Diaz Albertini. She testified that the county had two full-time crews assigned to pick up dead animals. But "the majority of the animals are cats and dogs," she said. "We get raccoons, we get armadillos, birds, all kinds of wild animals." They were more numerous than the carcasses of sacrificed animals, and none of the animals Albertini mentioned were animals sacrificed in Santeria rites.

Garrett therefore pressed ahead with his third main argument in support of Hialeah's ordinances. As he had claimed during his opening statement, ritual animal sacrifice is harmful to children. A prominent research psychologist specializing in the study of aggressive and violent behavior, Dr. L. Rowell Huesmann, was called to testify. Huesmann held a Ph.D. in communications science and psychology from Carnegie-Mellon University. He had taught briefly at Yale University before moving to the University of Illinois–Chicago. At the time, he was a rising academic star and emerging expert on violence in the media. A few years earlier, he had testified before the judiciary committees of both the U.S. Senate and the House of Representatives. In Judge Spellman's courtroom, he testified about the psychological harm to children caused by exposure to animal sacrifices.

Huesmann testified that Santeria initiation rites, which involve the sacrifice of a large number of animals, might detrimentally affect the mental health of children, especially if they are initiates. A child observing animal sacrifice would probably become more inclined toward aggressive and violent behavior as a result of three factors. First, they experience what psychologists term "desensitization" toward aggressive and violent acts. Second, by observing animal sacrifices, children might become more tolerant and accepting of such behavior. Third, the process of imitation — children imitating the behavior of adults and persons held in high regard — might contribute to aggressive and violent behavior. Although not claiming that children's behavior would necessarily be altered, Huesmann concluded, "you would have people who would be more likely to engage in violent acts as adults of a comparable population not exposed to the same scenes."

Duarte countered by calling two local witnesses: Dr. Angel Velez-Diaz, a clinical psychologist, and Joli Hendrix, a teacher of psychology at Miami-Dade Community College. Based on his treatment of clients, Velez-Diaz testified that "desensitization" toward violence would not necessarily result from children witnessing animal sacrifices. In the first place, priests or the children's families would undoubtedly prepare them psychologically. Second, other intervening factors might contribute to or better explain children's aggressive and violent behavior. Based on her study of children's attitudes toward death, Hendrix testified that those exposed to the death of animals might actually view death as a natural process. In her view, animal sacrifice was not a violent act per se or necessarily perceived as violence.

These two experts were clearly outgunned by Huesmann, and they left Judge Spellman completely unimpressed. He discounted Velez-Diaz's testimony, noting that he had never actually conducted any scientific studies of violent children, and dismissed Hendrix's testimony as hearsay and irrelevant. "First," observed Judge Spellman, "she is completely unfamiliar with the studies done by Dr. Huesmann. Second, her own research had to do with attitudes towards death, not violence. Third, she claimed no personal knowledge regarding how animals were sacrificed, nor did she claim to have any contact with children who had observed such sacrifices."

Duarte tried to rebut the claim that children of worshippers of Santeria suffer emotional and psychological harm. "What about Moses?" he asked, referring to the biblical figure's portrayal in the movie *The Ten Commandments*. "Children on farms? Viewers of Rambo and Dirty Harry? The superhero cartoons?"

Judge Spellman impatiently interrupted to say: "Don't give away what you do on Saturday mornings, Mr. Duarte." Not surprisingly, he had concluded that the allegedly harmful effects of animal sacrifice on children supported Hialeah's ordinances.

———

On August 28, 1989, Judge Spellman heard closing arguments in a little over two hours. Duarte tried to put the case into historical and political perspective, while Horwich reviewed the First Amendment claims and Rosen the Section 1983 claims. Garrett and Singer also divided their time in recounting their arguments about Hialeah's interests in the ordinances. No new arguments were made, but Duarte's argumentation and interaction with Judge Spellman were revealing.

After it was agreed that Duarte had twenty minutes to make his summation, he began with a sweeping and rather emotional overview of the persecution of followers of Santeria. "May it please the court, defense counsel," he began, "I don't know where to start talking about this case, Judge, other than to tell you it started somewhere in Africa and it started somewhere with blacks living there and with whites living in Europe." At that, Duarte launched into a long, rambling review of the history of slavery, the persecution of followers of Santeria in Cuba, and the exodus of Cubans to South Florida. He then turned to a lengthy discussion of animal cruelty laws and how humane society officials had used them to harass and persecute *santeros*.

Judge Spellman finally interrupted to ask: "Where is the evidence to establish what you just said?" Duarte replied: "Mr. Pichardo said it in his direct testimony at quite some length the degree of persecution, the prosecution and arrests that took place during the decade of the sixties and the seventies." However, Judge Spellman cut him off: "I don't recall him being rather — any specific." What followed was a sharp exchange that led the judge to observe: "You have set up an attack on the Humane Society." To this, Duarte responded, again, at length:

> It is not an attack on the Humane Society, what occurred here was an unholy marriage, an unholy alliance between the humane society and all those bigots and all those ethnocentrics that came over from Cuba and took the oath to become servants, public servants in the United States. That is what happened and all of their beliefs, all of their practices are reflected in these ordinances.
>
> They got together, two different forces, the ethnocentrics and the biocentrics and they joined forces in Hialeah and enacted a series of laws to prohibit the religious offering of animals. That occurred in the City of Hialeah. Those laws are unconstitutional and they are unworkable for many reasons because in their zeal to do these things, Judge, they have outlawed and have made it illegal for an owner in a restaurant to keep a live lobster in a tank. They have made it a crime for a high school student in Hialeah high school to dissect a live frog in a biology lab. They have made it illegal for all of the Hispanic residents to follow their annual traditions of killing a pig or killing a quail for Christmas. Yes, Judge, they have also made it a criminal offense for a citizen in the City of Hialeah to set a mousetrap or set on a cockroach. That is how these laws are unworkable. That is why these laws violate the Constitution of the United States, they have said you cannot kill any animal unless you have a license. . . .
>
> Judge, these people are no different today in South Florida than Jews were in Nazi Germany. These people are no different than Japanese-Americans living in the U.S. during World War II. They are no different than the United States blacks before the American civil rights movement. They're no different than the Catholics of Northern Ireland today and no different than the Palestinians that live in and around Jerusalem.

In his final few minutes, Duarte made his most emotional plea, threatening Judge Spellman: "If you don't believe me, Judge, if you think I am exaggerating, go ahead and rule for us. Declare those ordinances unconstitutional, give us monetary damages and you will see how you, yourself, the United States District Judge, will become the target of ridicule, will become the target of discrimination and will become the target of innuendo."

At that, Judge Spellman said simply: "Mr. Horwich. Have you and Mr. Rosen broken it up to twenty minutes each?" Once again, Spellman and Duarte were clearly not communicating. They were worlds apart.

Judge Spellman Renders His Ruling

Almost seven weeks passed before Judge Spellman handed down his decision on October 5, 1989. In a fifty-page opinion, he upheld all four ordinances. In his Findings of Fact, he reviewed the history of Afro-Caribbean religions and how Santeria came to be practiced in Cuba and South Florida. He stressed that "Santeria remains an underground religion and the practice was not, and is not today, socially accepted by the majority of the Cuban population." He also pointed out that other Afro-Caribbean religions sacrifice animals, making it difficult, if not impossible, to tell whether discarded animal carcasses are those left by followers of Santeria or other religions.

Within that context, Judge Spellman made much of Pichardo's testimony about the number of animals sacrificed in Santeria initiation rites. He estimated "that between 12,000 and 18,000 animals are sacrificed in initiation rites alone, during a one year period." Clearly, in his mind, that posed potentially serious health hazards when the remains of animals were left in public places.

Turning to the ordinances, Judge Spellman briefly reviewed the history of their adoption. Notably, he concluded that although they were "not religiously neutral but were to stop the practice of animal sacrifice in the City of Hialeah, the ordinances were not passed to interfere with religious beliefs, but rather to regulate conduct." He found that Hialeah's ordinances advanced "three compelling secular purposes: 1) to prevent the cruelty to animals; 2) to safeguard the health, welfare and safety of the community; and 3) to prevent the adverse psychological effect on children exposed to such sacrifices." As in his decision a year earlier, he found no evidence that Hialeah city officials or employees had discriminated against or harassed Ernesto Pichardo and the church.

In his Conclusions of Law, Judge Spellman dealt, first, with whether an actual controversy existed, whether Pichardo and the church had suffered a distinct and palpable injury giving them standing to sue. He was troubled by the fact that Pichardo and other members of the church had not been prosecuted. He also expressed concern that if he invalidated Hialeah's ordinances, Pichardo and the church would still be barred from performing animal sacrifices under state law and remain subject to (though they had not challenged) other ordinances pertaining to licensing, zoning, and health and sanitation regulations. Nonetheless, he concluded that he should rule on the claim that the ordinances infringed on religious freedom.

As for the constitutional challenge to the ordinances, Judge Spellman emphasized that, under the Supreme Court's rulings, the First Amendment's guarantees are not absolute. Paraphrasing Justice Oliver Wendell Holmes's famous observation that the guarantee of free speech does not protect an individual who shouts "fire" in a crowded theater and creates "a clear and present danger," Judge Spellman drew an analogy: "Freedom of religion, like freedom of speech, is subject to a similar analysis when we are dealing, as here, with the manner in which the religion is conducted rather than the beliefs of those seeking to exercise it. It is the former and not the latter which is the subject matter of this Court's opinion."

Having relegated the free exercise claim to one of freedom from the regulation of particular conduct, Judge Spellman reasoned that determining whether the ordinances were unconstitutional required balancing the competing governmental and religious interests. In balancing those interests, the ordinances had to pass two tests: Were they regulations of conduct, rather than of religious beliefs? And did they have a secular purpose and effect? Judge Spellman did not consider whether the city also had to advance its interests by the least drastic means, so as to accommodate religious minorities.

Judge Spellman had no doubt that Hialeah met both tests. According to him, the ordinances were indisputably directed at conduct, not belief; they merely proscribed ritual animal sacrifice. Unquestionably, the ordinances had a secular purpose and effect. The practice of discarding animal carcasses in public places was a growing problem, and the opening of the Church of the Lukumi had merely triggered the city council's enactment of ordinances to address that problem. Hialeah had a secular purpose in protecting the health and welfare of the community and in preventing animal cruelty.

The argument that the word *ritual* was synonymous with *religious* was rejected out of hand. Judge Spellman held that the city's prohibition of "ritual animal sacrifice" not only reaches "religious conduct, but also includes the killing of animals by groups that would probably not enjoy First Amendment protection, such as satanic cults." Further, he observed, "even if the use of the words 'ritual' and 'ceremony' are understood as targeting primarily religious conduct, nothing in the First Amendment prevents a municipality from specifically regulating such conduct when it is deemed inconsistent with public health and welfare."

Admittedly, Hialeah's ordinances burdened the practice of Santeria. But in balancing the competing interests, Judge Spellman concluded that the church's First Amendment claims were outweighed by the city's interests in safeguarding public health, preventing adverse psychological effects on children exposed to such sacrifices, and preventing animal cruelty.

First, with respect to the city's interest in combating the health hazards, he noted that other federal and state courts had upheld bans on the handling of poisonous snakes and the smoking of marijuana, in spite of claims that those activities were central to certain religions. Hialeah more than met its burden of showing a substantial health risk from the killing of animals in areas other than slaughterhouses, since "animal carcasses are often left in public places, leading to an increased risk of disease. Additionally, the animals are often obtained from sources that have not maintained the animals in sanitary conditions; nor have the animals gone through any inspection process. This is especially dangerous," he emphasized, "when dealing with chickens, due to the increased risk of salmonella."

Second, Judge Spellman concluded, "the governmental interest in guaranteeing the welfare of children is particularly strong." Based on the expert testimony presented, he ruled, "the City has shown that the risk to children justifies the absolute ban on animal sacrifice."

Finally, Hialeah's interest in protecting animals from cruelty and unnecessary killing was deemed compelling. Judge Spellman granted

Duarte's argument that the killing of animals is not inhumane in itself, but he found more persuasive the expert testimony of Dr. Fox. Judge Spellman agreed that the method used by Santeria priests in sacrificing animals was unreliable and not humane. Again, he stressed, "the animals perceive both pain and fear during the actual sacrificial ceremony," in part because prior to the ritual they "are kept in filthy, overcrowded conditions, and sometimes not given adequate food or water."

In concluding, Judge Spellman briefly considered the argument that the free exercise clause requires an exemption for the church's practice of ritual animal sacrifice. He dismissed that claim out of hand. Pichardo had testified that if the church were allowed to openly practice animal sacrifice, it would conform to the city's other regulations, thereby setting an example for other practitioners of Santeria and animal sacrifice. But Judge Spellman rejected that as mere speculation "without any factual support." It appeared unworkable as well. Not all followers of Santeria belonged to the Church of the Lukumi, and there was no guarantee that those who practiced Voodoo or other religions would adhere to the city's regulations. "Most importantly," he stressed, "the carving out of an exception for any group would defeat the City's valid and compelling interests." Any "exception would have to cover all religions." A religious exception, he concluded, "would, in effect, swallow the rule."

Judge Spellman thus ruled that Hialeah's ordinances passed constitutional muster. They did not target the Church of the Lukumi or Santeria. Instead, they simply prohibited all ritual animal sacrifice. In doing so, they advanced the city's legitimate interests, and any exception for religious minorities would defeat those interests.

––––––––

Judge Spellman's decision was a bitter defeat for the church. Pichardo, Duarte, and others associated with the case never doubted that they would appeal. At the time, Duarte told reporters: "It is a dark day for religious freedom. We've made criminals out of 70,000 people in South Florida." The ACLU's Mitchell Horwich promised to appeal, reaffirming: "Their right to practice this faith is protected by [the] First Amendment and these rights outweigh the interests of the city in stopping it."

CHAPTER 5

Conflicting Cultures

Mitchell Horwich, Maurice Rosen, and others with the Miami chapter of the ACLU knew they needed assistance in appealing Judge Spellman's ruling. Specifically, they needed someone with appellate experience, because appellate advocacy is different from arguing in a trial court. Stephen R. Shapiro of the ACLU's national office and Mark Stern of the American Jewish Congress suggested Douglas Laycock. Shapiro knew of his work, and Stern had met him a year earlier at a conference at the University of Notre Dame School of Law. As a result, Laycock was recruited to take the lead on the appeal.

Laycock, a professor at the University of Texas School of Law in Austin, appeared ideally suited. He had experience in both constitutional law and appellate advocacy. After graduating from the University of Chicago School of Law, he had clerked for Judge Walter J. Cummings on the Seventh Circuit Court of Appeals. During a decade at the University of Texas, he had published articles on constitutional law, including religious freedom, in leading law reviews such as the *Harvard Law Review, Columbia Law Review*, and *Supreme Court Review*. He had also argued several cases before federal appellate courts.

Laycock served as counsel for the National Council of Churches and had recently drafted an amicus curiae brief for a wide spectrum of groups in opposition to the ruling in *Oregon v. Smith*. The lineup included the American Jewish Congress, American Jewish Committee, ACLU, Americans United for the Separation of Church and State, Baptist Joint Committee for Public Affairs, Catholic League for Religious and Civil Rights, Evangelical Lutheran Church in America, General Conference of Seventh-day Adventists, National Association of Evangelicals, National Council of Churches of Christ in the USA, People for the American Way, Unitarian Universalist Association,

Williamsburg Charter Foundation, and Worldwide Church of God. Laycock's brief was to have been filed in support of a petition asking the justices for a rehearing on *Oregon v. Smith*, which he had signed as well, along with a number of other prominent law professors, including former congressman Robert F. Drinan from Georgetown University and Harvard professor Laurence H. Tribe. But shortly after sending his brief to the printer, Laycock discovered that in 1990 the Court had amended its rules for such submissions. Because more and more interest groups were seeking to influence the Court's decisions, it now forbade the filing of amicus briefs in support of petitions for the rehearing of cases. Like most such requests, the petition for a rehearing of *Oregon v. Smith* was simply denied. Although the change in the Court's rules precluded Laycock's filing of his amicus brief, he published it as an article in the *Journal of Law and Religion* in 1990. The title reflected his uncompromising position: "The Supreme Court's Assault on Free Exercise, and the Amicus Brief That Was Never Filed."

———

In the Eleventh Circuit

Federal appellate courts usually operate with panels of three judges who are assigned cases on a rotating basis. There are eleven circuits geographically dividing the country, plus the U.S. Court of Appeals for the District of Columbia Circuit and the Court of Appeals for the Federal Circuit. Each has between six and twenty-eight judges, depending on its caseload. Only in exceptional cases, when two or more panels render conflicting rulings, does the entire circuit court meet to decide cases. Notably, less than 1 percent of all appeals of circuit court decisions are granted by the Supreme Court. Federal appellate courts thus play the role of "mini Supreme Courts."

Judge Spellman's decision was appealed to the Court of Appeals for the Eleventh Circuit, whose jurisdiction extends over Alabama, Georgia, and Florida. At the time, it was one of the most conservative federal appellate courts, dominated by appointees of Republican presidents. As it turned out, the three-judge panel assigned to hear the appeal was composed of stereotypical "old-time southern judges."

The panel consisted of Judge Peter T. Fay, a sixty-one-year-old

Catholic from Miami. He had been appointed to the federal district court in 1970 by Nixon and elevated in 1976 by Ford. Judge Emmett Ripley Cox was fifty-five, an Alabaman who had earned his undergraduate and law degrees from the University of Alabama. Reagan had named him to an Alabama district court in 1981 and elevated him to the appellate bench in 1988. They were joined by a seventy-year-old judge on senior status, Judge Albert J. Henderson. Unlike Fay and Cox, he was a Georgia Democrat, appointed to the bench in 1968 by Johnson and elevated in 1981 by Carter.

The oral arguments before the Eleventh Circuit panel pitted Laycock against Garrett for the first time. Although they were not particularly remarkable, Laycock recalled being surprised that Judge Fay asked virtually no questions, yet he had rigorously questioned the attorneys during the preceding case that day. It fell largely to Judge Cox to ask a few questions. Judge Henderson made a couple of cracks about breaking the necks of chickens while growing up on a farm in Georgia.

More remarkable was that after the case was submitted, the attorneys heard nothing for six months. Laycock speculated that the court might have been trying to draft an opinion justifying its decision in light of *Oregon v. Smith*, which had come down the preceding June. When the Supreme Court hands down a major decision, appellate courts usually try to incorporate and apply the new ruling in pertinent cases.

Almost a month before the Eleventh Circuit panel issued its decision, Judge Spellman died of cancer at age sixty, on May 4, 1991. He was mourned by the local Haitian community and the Dade County Bar Association as a "great jurist." In the press, he was remembered for the Haitian refugee decision, innovative sentencing, and his support for social causes, along with his ruling on animal sacrifices.

Rather surprisingly, on June 11, 1991, the Eleventh Circuit issued a one-paragraph, unsigned, per curiam opinion affirming Judge Spellman's decision. Although the court affirmed his conclusions of law and his holding that Hialeah's ordinances were consistent with the First Amendment, it set aside his conclusion that Hialeah had a compelling interest in combating the allegedly harmful consequences for children exposed to animal sacrifice.

In a footnote, the panel noted that Judge Spellman "employed an arguably stricter standard in analyzing whether the ordinances violate the United States Constitution than the Supreme Court did in *Employment Div., Dept. of Human Resources v. Smith.*" But, the panel added, "we need not decide the effect of *Smith* in this case." No further explanation was given. The Eleventh Circuit did not publish the opinion, perhaps because of its brevity and because of the trend begun in the 1980s of federal appellate courts not publishing all their opinions owing to their growing caseloads.

Animal rights supporters were elated by the circuit's ruling. The Humane Society of the United States applauded the decision for raising "to a national level the HSUS's position that the U.S. Constitution does not protect animal cruelty as a religious practice." Marc Paulhus declared: "Religious practice and religious belief are not the same thing. By the most conservative estimates, there are a quarter of a million Santeria practitioners in the U.S. These people are certainly entitled to their religious beliefs. They are not, however, entitled to perpetrate cruelty to animals for the sake of these beliefs."

————

Pichardo, Duarte, Laycock, and the ACLU attorneys were disappointed. Moreover, the odds of the Supreme Court granting a review of the appeal were not very promising. Although Americans often say "I will take my case all the way to the Supreme Court," few actually get a hearing.

For one thing, at the end of the Court's 1989–1990 term, just a little over a month after *Oregon v. Smith* was handed down, Justice Brennan retired. Considered one of the most liberal and influential justices in the twentieth century, he had authored *Sherbert v. Verner*, which *Oregon v. Smith* abandoned. His vote would be missed.

Justice Brennan was replaced on the bench by Justice David H. Souter. At the time, little was known about him, and few could have foreseen that he would emerge as a fierce defender of religious freedom and side with liberal justices on the Rehnquist Court. At age fifty, Souter was the same age Justice Brennan had been when he joined the high court. Souter had been a Rhodes scholar at Oxford University and received his law degree from Harvard. He served as New Hampshire's attorney general, later became a state supreme court justice, and sat for a short time on a federal appellate court. Three days of testimony before the Senate Judiciary Committee on his nomination revealed more about the senators than about him. He strove to disabuse the notions that his rural New Hampshire background, solitariness, and bookish lifestyle boded ill for the Court or the country. Unlike the ill-fated and controversial nominee Robert Bork, Souter was reticent to explain his views on controversial issues. Throughout his testimony, Souter reassured senators that he had no agenda or rigid philosophy of interpreting the Constitution. The "majestic clauses" of the Constitution were broad, requiring attention to history and precedent as well as to the text. By a vote of thirteen to one, the Senate Judiciary Committee recommended confirmation. Justice Souter was then confirmed by a vote of ninety to nine on October 2, 1990.

Besides the uncertainty about Justice Souter, there were other more pressing factors in the decision whether to appeal. In light of *Oregon v. Smith*, the prospects of winning in the Court did not look good. Some attorneys and law professors urged the ACLU not to take the case to the highest court in the land. Given *Oregon v. Smith*, an appeal might simply be dismissed as frivolous.

At the time, a disturbing trend at the Court was also becoming apparent. Although the number of appeals was steadily climbing, the Rehnquist Court was granting review to fewer cases. In the 1990 term, the Court had 6,316 cases on its docket; in the 1989 term, there had been 5,746 cases, and 5,657 in the 1988 term. Yet only 125 cases were granted plenary consideration — that is, full briefing and oral arguments — which was down from 146 in 1989 and 170 in 1988. As it turned out, during the 1991–1992 term, just 112 cases were granted review from a docket of 6,770 cases, a little more than 1 percent. Pichardo and his attorneys knew that the odds were against them.

To make matters worse, less than a month after the Eleventh Circuit handed down its ruling, the last predictable liberal justice, Thurgood Marshall, announced that he would retire after twenty-four years on the bench. He was a larger-than-life metaphor for the civil rights movement, the first black to sit on the Court, and the last appointee of a Democratic president. As a young attorney, he had led the National Association for the Advancement of Colored People Legal Defense Fund and had successfully argued a companion case to the watershed school desegregation case, *Brown v. Board of Education of*

Topeka, Kansas. LBJ subsequently made him solicitor general and then elevated him to the Court in 1967.

Four days later, on July 1, 1991, President George H. W. Bush nominated Justice Marshall's successor, Judge Clarence Thomas. Just fifteen months earlier, Bush had named him to fill Bork's seat on the Court of Appeals for the District of Columbia Circuit. Despite the president's denial that Thomas was "a quota" and his defense of him as "the best man for the job on the merits," Thomas's qualifications were immediately questioned. At age forty-three, he was one of the youngest ever to join the Court; the average age of the preceding 105 justices was a full decade older.

More than his qualifications sparked controversy, however. During his testimony before the Senate Judiciary Committee, he repeatedly emphasized his up-by-the-bootstraps philosophy and personal struggle to overcome the poverty of his youth. After almost two weeks of hearings, the committee was deadlocked. Split seven to seven over whether to recommend confirmation, it voted thirteen to one to send his nomination to the full Senate without a recommendation. Then, new allegations arose: former assistant Anita F. Hill claimed that he had sexually harassed her a decade earlier when he was chair of the Equal Employment Opportunity Commission. Amid growing public anger over the accusations and countercharges, the Judiciary Committee held hearings pitting Hill against Thomas. Hill confidently claimed that Thomas had sexually harassed her, frequently talked about pornographic movies, and created a hostile work environment. Thomas categorically denied the accusations, angrily protesting that the confirmation process had become a "high-tech lynching for uppity blacks." The nasty drama of "she said, he said" failed to resolve the controversy. At the end of another week of fighting, the Senate voted fifty-two to forty-eight to confirm him.

———

One night after the appeal was filed, Duarte went to Pichardo's house. He told him that although everything possible had been done to get the case accepted, ACLU attorneys reported that professors at Harvard Law School and elsewhere felt that the chances of having it granted were slim. They thought this not only because the Rehnquist

Court was granting review to fewer cases but also because it was too soon after *Oregon v. Smith* for the justices to take another case dealing with religious minorities.

Duarte also told Pichardo that some lawyers and law professors had said that even if the Supreme Court accepted the case, "you'll probably lose." *Oregon v. Smith* did not bode well for the church's case or for religious minorities. "It might be best to leave it the way it is," Duarte reported.

Pichardo told Duarte: "You've trusted, very strangely, for some weird reason, you've believed in me when I said we are going to win this case. Remember, I couldn't even pay you. For some reason, you trusted me. When we went to the trial, you asked what is going to happen? I said that I didn't like it, but we are going to win, this is a process. We are going through a process. We are going to go through several stages. Jorge, trust me again. The *orishas* say we are going to win, we are a winner."

"Look at this way," Pichardo further explained, "it is going to affect every religion. Look at what this stupid little chicken thing has become. Look at the responsibility on our backs. It is no longer just us, it is everybody. So, I don't care what these mental giants at Harvard say. It may be a conservative Court, but these judges aren't idiots. And this is the only court that can look at the case and objectively see right through it. Everything else that was done in Florida is politics. Let's get it up there and finish the process, like the *orishas* have been saying. We have nothing to lose and plenty to gain for everyone."

The Court Grants Review, Interest Groups Mobilize

Months later, on Monday, March 23, 1992, the Court announced that the *Church of Lukumi Babalu Aye, Inc., and Ernesto Pichardo v. City of Hialeah*, docket number 91-948, was granted. The case was scheduled for oral arguments at the beginning of the October 1992 term. In the meantime, counsel on both sides would prepare and file briefs on the merits, presenting their legal arguments on the questions at issue. Interest groups on both sides also immediately mobilized to file friend-of-the-court briefs.

Along with the church's and Hialeah's briefs, there were ten amicus curiae briefs filed. Originally, amicus curiae briefs merely brought arguments and data not in the main briefs to the Court's attention, but they are no longer neutral or friendly. They are partisan, permitting interest groups to enter litigation as third parties. In the leading affirmative action case of *Regents of the University of California v. Bakke* (1978), 120 organizations joined 58 briefs: 83 for the University of California at Davis in support of its affirmative action program for admission into its medical school, 32 in support of Allan Bakke's challenge to the constitutionality of the program, and 5 urging the Court not to decide the case. The number of briefs filed in *Bakke* was exceeded a decade later during the abortion controversy in *Webster v. Reproductive Health Services* (1989), in which a record 78 amicus curiae briefs were filed.

It remains unclear how influential such briefs are, for they may or may not be cited. Much depends on the issues, the case, and the justices. When a large number are filed, some justices have their law clerks screen and divide them according to which they should "read, skim, or skip." In *Webster,* the briefs on both sides clearly helped shape the debate within the Court. The justices cited twenty-nine separate amicus briefs, several more than once, for a total of forty-three citations. The large number of briefs filed and cited in *Webster* was extraordinary, although in the last half of the twentieth century, the trend was toward more citations in the justices' opinions.

Although not as controversial as affirmative action or abortion, the church's case mobilized a broad coalition of religious organizations in support of the church. They were squarely at odds with organized interest groups devoted to animal rights. Four amicus briefs, joined by nineteen organizations, were filed in support the church. They aimed not only to defend religious freedom but also, more specifically, to persuade the Court to reconsider and limit or overrule *Oregon v. Smith* and reestablish *Sherbert v. Verner.* Five briefs, joined by eighteen organizations, supported Hialeah; all these organizations and groups were committed to the advancement of animal rights. One brief, filed by the U.S. Catholic Conference, supported neither side.

The leading amicus brief in support of the church was filed by Americans United for Separation of Church and State, a nonprofit umbrella organization with some 50,000 members known for championing religious freedom. The brief was joined by the American Jewish Committee, founded in 1906 to protect the civil and religious rights of Jews; the American Jewish Congress, founded in 1918 and a frequent participant in lawsuits defending free exercise claims; the Anti-Defamation League of B'nai B'rith, which was founded in 1913 to advance the religious understanding of all Americans; the Baptist Joint Committee on Public Affairs; the Catholic League for Religious and Civil Rights; the Christian Legal Society, representing 4,500 Christian judges and lawyers; the Church of Jesus Christ of Latter-day Saints, whose membership includes 4 million people and more than 9,000 congregations; the Evangelical Lutheran Church in America; the First Liberty Institute at George Mason University; the General Conference of Seventh-day Adventists; the Home School Legal Defense Association; the Mennonite Central Committee of the United States; the National Association of Evangelicals; the People for the American Way, a liberal organization founded in 1980 with over 300,000 members; and the clerk of the General Assembly of the Presbyterian Church.

Three other briefs were filed by the National Jewish Commission on Law and Public Affairs; the Council on Religious Freedom, a non-profit organization devoted to religious freedom; and the Rutherford Institute, a nonprofit research and litigation organization based in Charlottesville, Virginia, associated with New Christian Right causes but also with strong libertarian positions.

In opposition was a brief filed by the Humane Society of the United States. Its brief was joined by the American Humane Association, the American Society for the Prevention of Cruelty to Animals, the Animal Legal Defense Fund, and the Massachusetts Society for the Prevention of Cruelty to Animals. Another brief was filed by the People for the Ethical Treatment of Animals (PETA), the New Jersey Animal Rights Alliance, and the Foundation for Animal Rights Advocacy. Two others were filed by the Washington Humane Society and the International Society for Animal Rights, along with Citizens for Animals and the Farm Animal Reform Movement.

Finally, the fifth brief in support of Hialeah was submitted by the Institute for Animal Rights Law. It was joined by five other organizations: the American Fund for Alternatives to Animal Research, Farm Sanctuary, Jews for Animal Rights, United Animal Nations, and United Poultry Concerns. Although this brief supported Hialeah, these groups urged the Court to dismiss the case or, in the parlance of the justices, to "DIG" (dismiss as improvidently granted) it.

———

The brief for the Americans United for Separation of Church and State was written principally by conservative law school professor Michael W. McConnell. McConnell had clerked for Justice Brennan after graduating from law school and then taught at the University of Chicago School of Law before joining the University of Utah College of Law. He had a reputation as a leading authority on the religion clauses and as a champion of conservative causes. In 1990, he published an important article criticizing *Oregon v. Smith* in the *Harvard Law Review* entitled "The Origins and Historical Understanding of Free Exercise of Religion," which several of the other amicus briefs cited. At the time, though, he worried that "the facts [in the church's case] are so unpleasant that the Court could lurch in the direction of minimizing free exercise rights."

In his brief, McConnell made four key points. First, animal sacrifice was an ancient religious practice. Santeria's practice was "virtually indistinguishable with the practices of animal sacrifice mentioned throughout the Bible." Early Jews and Christians sacrificed animals, at least until the Romans destroyed the Second Temple in 70 C.E. Christians then abandoned animal sacrifices for theological reasons, due to the ascendance of "the view that further sacrifice was rendered forever unnecessary by the ultimate sacrifice of the pure lamb of God on the cross at Calvary."

Second, the appellate court had ignored the Court's doctrines requiring governmental neutrality toward religion. Third, Judge Spellman had expressly found that the ordinances were "not religiously neutral but were intended to stop the practice of animal sacrifice in Hialeah," yet he had upheld them as advancing the government's interests. In other words, both lower courts had improperly applied the Court's requirement that governmental interests infringing on the free exercise of religion be both compelling and the least drastic means of achieving its goals.

Fourth, McConnell contended that *Oregon v. Smith* had been wrongly decided. No less important, *Smith* had been misapplied by lower federal courts. For example, lower courts had enforced laws requiring autopsies over the objections of Orthodox Jews, for whom the defilement of the body is a sacrilege. Unless *Smith* was corrected, the Court and the country faced the proverbial parade of horribles. As McConnell elaborated:

> Roman Catholic children will no longer have a right of excusal from sex education classes in public schools contrary to their religious teaching; no longer will churches have a free exercise right of exemption from employment laws forbidding discrimination against homosexuals when they choose their minister or music director; no longer will doctors or nurses be able to assert a religious ground for declining to participate in compulsory training or participation in abortion procedures; no longer will the confidentiality of the confessional be constitutionally protected when prosecutors call the priest as a witness in court; no longer will Jewish prisoners be entitled to kosher meals; no longer will religious schools be able to invoke the Free Exercise Clause to shield themselves from accreditation standards applicable to secular public schools; no longer can Jehovah's Witnesses avoid jury service, can Christian Scientists avoid unwanted medical care, or Jewish college students avoid exams scheduled on high holidays. All these are relegated to their political remedies, despite the manifest tendency of the political process to favor the mainstream over the heterodox.

Finally, McConnell implored "the Court to be aware of the practical consequences of constitutional rules that turn a blind eye toward the realities of official treatment of unfamiliar and unpopular religious groups, particularly at the local level."

The brief for the National Jewish Commission on Law and Public Affairs focused on the specific problems confronting Orthodox Jews in light of *Oregon v. Smith*. It was written by Nathan Lewin, a prominent attorney in the District of Columbia and frequent litigator of free exercise claims. If the lower courts' decisions were not reversed, he argued, the Court would "jeopardize the availability of kosher food in the United States. Meat and poultry is kosher only if derived from an animal slaughtered in accordance with rabbinic requirements that have been obligatory upon Jews for more than two thousand years — i.e., by the prescribed Jewish ritual method of *shehitah*."

Lewin's brief reminded the justices that the first anti-Jewish laws enacted in 1933 in Nazi Germany under Adolf Hitler were laws out-lawing *shehitah* on the grounds that it was cruel to animals. Hialeah's ordinances were not generally applicable laws. Rather, they targeted conduct "engaged in for religious reasons" and therefore were uncon-stitutional. Even under *Smith*, the most compelling governmental interest was completely immaterial if a law directly discriminated against conduct "engaged in for religious reasons." Thus, there was no escaping the fundamental conflict between freedom of religion and animal rights. Lewin took strong exception with Judge Spellman's conclusion that the prevention of cruelty to animals was a compelling interest overriding religious convictions. As he put it: "Requiring a person to violate divine commands that govern his conscience is exceedingly 'cruel' to a human being. A municipality's interest in pre-venting 'cruelty' to an animal is, we submit, inadequate to justify per-petrating 'cruelty' on sincere conscientious believers."

Whereas Lewin's brief focused on the problems posed for Ortho-dox Jews by *Oregon v. Smith*, the brief for the Council on Religious Freedom took *Smith* on more broadly. It urged the justices "to over-rule or severely limit application of its decision in *Smith*, [and] reverse the judgment of the court of appeals" affirming Judge Spellman's rul-ing. *Smith* was "calamitous" in bringing "confusion, rather than clar-ity, to free exercise jurisprudence." The brief concluded by highlighting a lengthy quote from a 1990 article by Laycock, "The Remnants of Free Exercise," published in the *Supreme Court Review*. There, much more sharply than in his brief now before the Court, Laycock had derided Justice Scalia's analysis in *Oregon v. Smith*:

> The [*Smith*] opinion's talk of centrality as a threshold requirement is thus a manufactured difficulty. But the Court is right that any balancing in the free exercise context must consider the burden on religious exercise as well as the threat to government's compelling interests. The Court says it would be unworkable to deny that point, for to deny it would require "the same degree of 'compelling state interest' to impede the practice of throwing rice at church weddings as to impede the practice of getting married in church." But of course no one ever denied the point, and the Court's *reducto ad absurdum* boomerangs. The majority appears to say it would be "horrible" and inappropriate for judges to recognize the differences

between throwing rice and getting married in church. I think they could handle it.

The Rutherford Institute adopted a somewhat more conciliatory, though still critical, approach to *Oregon v. Smith*. It maintained that *Smith*'s "generally applicable, facially religion-neutral" formulation did not control the case here. It appeared to give the justices a break in pointing out that "*Smith* does not unambiguously represent this Court's definitive adoption of a complete reordering of a body of law that took forty years to develop." The Rutherford Institute thus offered the Court a way out of the controversy. It could reexamine the history of the free exercise clause and reassert "solicitude for the role of religion as a mediating institution in culture," "fidelity to constitutional text," and "the conservative instinct to proceed cautiously on a case-by-case basis." Accordingly, the Court was urged to "reverse the judgment below on the basis that the ordinances had an invidious discriminatory purpose in violation of both the Free Exercise and Establishment Clauses. In the alternative," the Court could "specifically set aside the conclusion of law that the City had compelling reasons for its ordinances. Then the case should be remanded with directions to hold a new trial (or reopen the judgment and receive further evidence)."

The briefs in support of the church aimed to engage the justices in a dialogue — a dialogue about constitutional principles and the freedom of religious minorities, as well as the consequences for state and local governments in following the ruling in *Oregon v. Smith*. They offered the justices a variety of alternatives for deciding the case in the favor of the Church of the Lukumi. The Court could simply distinguish *Smith*, limit its reach, or reconsider and overrule it.

———

Joining the dialogue with the Court were the briefs filed in support of Hialeah's ordinances by animal rights groups. Not surprisingly, the brief for the Humane Society of the United States contended that the ordinances were neutral, generally applicable laws advancing the city's interest in preventing animal cruelty. It underscored that Justice Scalia in *Oregon v. Smith* had cited Judge Spellman's decision as an example of courts' upholding laws of general applicability that serve governmental interests in public health and animal welfare. It repeatedly emphasized the correctness of his suggestion that Hialeah's ordinances were "not meant to single out persons engaged in ritual sacrifice, but to put those persons on notice that the state exemption for ritual slaughter only applied to commercial ritual slaughter, done in slaughterhouses."

The Humane Society further countered that the use of the words *ritual, ceremony,* and *sacrifice* in the ordinances was neutral, not explicitly religious, as Laycock claimed. In its view:

> The word "sacrifice" is also religiously neutral. Contrary to petitioners' claim that "sacrifice is an explicitly religious practice," the word "sacrifice" is expressly defined in neutral terms in the ordinances. Whatever meaning "sacrifice" may have in the abstract is irrelevant. Thus, as the plain meaning of the ordinances confirms, Hialeah does not ban sacrifices "only when they are engaged in for religious reasons, or only because of the religious belief that they display" [quoting *Oregon v. Smith*]; animal sacrifice is banned altogether as inconsistent with the community's values.

Likewise, the brief submitted by PETA argued that *Smith* rejected "a private right to ignore generally applicable laws" and defended the ordinances as neutral and generally applicable. Its brief drove home, again, the fact that Justice Scalia's opinion in *Smith* appeared to endorse Hialeah's ordinances. According to PETA, *Smith* had already settled the matter. The Court should affirm the lower courts and uphold Hialeah's ordinances.

A third brief was filed by the Washington Humane Society, but most of its arguments were repetitive. It agreed that the ordinances were neutral and generally applicable, that they were neither overly broad nor unconstitutionally vague. They did not target a particular religion, and they advanced compelling governmental interests in preventing animal cruelty. However, the Washington Humane Society belabored the argument that animal sacrifice might contribute to children's aggressive and violent behavior. Highlighting the trial testimony of expert witnesses, the brief asserted: "The evidence at trial established that exposure to the ritual sacrifice of animals imperils the psychological well-being of children and increases the likelihood that a child will become more aggressive and violent. Based on the expert testimony, the City has shown that the risk to children justifies the absolute ban on animal sacrifice."

Still another brief was filed by the International Society for Animal Rights, along with other supporting organizations. In some respects, it was more daring than the other briefs. It urged the Court to abandon its "compelling governmental interest" test for governmental regulations altogether and to substitute the lower "heightened scrutiny" test for the more rigorous "strict scrutiny" test when evaluating religious claims. Governments had important and legitimate interests in constraining religious practices such as animal sacrifice. Moreover, in its view, *Sherbert v. Verner* had been wrongly decided in the first place. *Sherbert* was mistaken in its accommodation of religious minorities by requiring regulations to advance a compelling governmental interest by the least drastic means. In short, generally applicable laws, such as those in all fifty states outlawing animal cruelty, should override any and all religious objections.

––––––

The two final amicus briefs were a bit unusual. One, filed by the Institute for Animal Rights Law, a New York–based nonprofit organization devoted to advancing the rights of animals, asked the Court not to decide the case. The other, filed by the U.S. Catholic Conference, supported neither side but deemed *Oregon v. Smith* a disaster and ill-considered judicial activism.

The brief submitted by the Institute for Animal Rights Law was written by Henry Mark Holzer and was joined by a range of other groups concerned with different aspects of animal cruelty. The American Fund for Alternatives to Animal Research, for instance, financially supports scientists developing non-animal-based scientific research and testing. Farm Sanctuary, a nonprofit organization of about 10,000 members formed in 1986, addresses the problems associated with "food animal" production. Jews for Animal Rights, founded in 1985, continues a tradition of *tsa'ar ba'alei chaim* ("remember the pain of living creatures") and promotes vegetarianism. The United Animal Nations, also founded in 1985, promotes the humane treatment of animals by orchestrating national protests, including putting animal exploiters "on trial." Finally, United Poultry Concerns combats abuses of domestic fowl in food production, science, and entertainment.

Somewhat surprisingly, given the common concerns uniting these groups, they urged the Court to dismiss the case as improvidently granted. They contended, on the one hand, that the case was not "ripe." It was not timely because Hialeah's ordinances had never actually been enforced against Pichardo and the church. Also, the church's application to slaughter animals, filed just two weeks before the trial started, had never been acted on. Pichardo and the church therefore had not suffered a personal injury and had no standing to sue. Moreover, even if the ordinances were invalidated, ritual animal sacrifices would still be prohibited under Florida's state law against animal cruelty.

On the other hand, Holzer argued that the case was moot. There was no longer a real case or controversy because the facts had changed. Holzer underscored that although animal sacrifice was something the church had planned to engage in when it initially opened at 173 West Fifth Street, when the church moved to 700 Palm Avenue prior to the trial, it publicly took the position that it would not perform animal sacrifices there. Pichardo had testified at the trial that the church was solely devoted to education, and he had acknowledged that under zoning regulations it could not perform animal sacrifices at its new location. Pichardo therefore no longer had a personal stake in the outcome of the case. In Holzer's words: "For, precisely because the 'church' can now most accurately be characterized as an academic Santeria think tank, with the 'priest' Pichardo as its chief academician, the question of whether petitioners can constitutionally be forbidden from sacrificing animals in Hialeah is an academic one, which fails to present a 'case or controversy.'"

In sum, the brief for the Institute for Animal Rights Law gave the justices another (not unreasonable) way out and set it apart from the other animal rights groups. In urging the justices to dismiss the case, the institute advanced a strategic preemptive effort at damage control. If the Court ruled for the church, its decision would stand as a major, perhaps insurmountable, obstacle to the further development of animal rights law. The Institute for Animal Rights Law aimed to prevent or at least minimize the prospects of that happening.

Finally, the brief for the U.S. Catholic Conference supported neither side. It was written by the conference's general counsel, Mark E. Chopko. It contended that more was at stake than which side won— "whether either side is ultimately right about the level of scrutiny, or who has the burden of proof." What was crucial was the direction of free exercise jurisprudence, the overruling of *Oregon v. Smith*, and the restoration of the protection afforded religious minorities under *Sherbert v. Verner.*

The Catholic Conference considered Justice Scalia's opinion in *Oregon v. Smith* an unmitigated disaster. "This Court should not permit its Free Exercise jurisprudence to continue to develop along the lines suggested in *Smith*," Chopko argued. "To do so disservices the purposes of the Bill of Rights and the constitutional protection it affords individuals, their organizations, and communities of faith. To do so would ultimately prove more frustrating to the Court and to religious communities, whose basic practices are now susceptible to restriction. It is not too soon to begin the process of confining *Smith* to its facts and begin a new commitment to the protection of religion."

Ironically, in the view of the Catholic Conference and many scholars, Justice Scalia, a Catholic known for advocating adherence to the "original intent" of the framers of the Constitution, had ignored the history and purpose of the First Amendment's free exercise clause. In the conference's view, Justice Scalia also drew the wrong balance between governmental interests and those of religious minorities: "In a clash between the dictates of conscience and the dictates of government, the individual religious conscience is to be given the benefit of every doubt." Contrary to what Justice Scalia had said in *Smith* about the preference of deferring to the operation of majoritarian democracy, the Catholic Conference maintained:

> Religion is a preferred constitutional value, entitled to benevolent treatment by the government, including this Court. Certainly, in light of *Smith*, religion deserves better treatment than it is now receiving at the hands of courts and legislatures throughout the United States. Because religion matters, those who would curtail religious activity should bear the burden of showing why it must be regulated. The government should be required to demonstrate a narrowly drawn and significant compelling interest to justify inroads on religion.

In addition, *Smith* was not merely confused about the history and principles of free exercise of religion but also confusing in its application. Like some other briefs, the Catholic Conference emphasized that after *Smith*, lower federal court rulings "resulted in a more thoroughgoing rejection of religious claims than had existed in the previous twenty years." In short, *Oregon v. Smith* should be overturned and *Sherbert v. Verner* resurrected.

The Battle of Briefs

Whether any influence was exerted by the friendly and not-so-friendly amicus briefs filed by the religious organizations and animal rights groups is impossible to gauge precisely. Only Justices Blackmun and O'Connor in a concurring opinion mentioned those filed by animal rights groups. Although they declined to reach "the question whether the Free Exercise Clause would require a religious exemption from a law that sincerely pursued the goal of protecting animals from cruel treatment," they noted that the number of animal rights groups filing and joining amicus briefs demonstrated that it was "not a concern to be treated lightly."

Undoubtedly more influential were the briefs filed and subsequent oral arguments by Laycock and Garrett. In his briefs filed before the Court, Laycock was joined by Duarte, Stephen R. Shapiro of the national office of the ACLU, Nine E. Vinik of the ACLU's Florida branch, Mitchell Horwich, and Jeanne Baker of Baker and Moscowitz. Garrett was assisted by Stuart H. Singer and Stephen M. Goldsmith, both from his law firm.

Laycock emphasized that Pichardo and the church were not challenging the ordinances banning the inhumane slaughter or torture of animals, only those outlawing ritual animal sacrifice. These ordinances directly targeted religious beliefs and practices "by expressly prohibiting 'sacrifice' and 'ritual' killings of animals, by the theological judgment that animal sacrifice is 'unnecessary,' and by religious gerrymanders based on primary and secondary purposes for killing of animals for religious purposes without forbidding the killing of animals for any plausible secular purpose." Highlighting the discriminatory purpose and effect of the ordinances, Laycock reminded the Court of Justice O'Connor's observation, concurring in *Oregon v. Smith*, that "few states would be so naive as to enact a law directly prohibiting or burdening a religious practice as such." Yet, he argued, that was "exactly what Hialeah has done here."

The crux of Laycock's argument was that any law burdening the free exercise of religion must at least be neutral and generally applicable. *Oregon v. Smith* held that a neutral, generally applicable law may override religiously motivated activities, but *Smith* also gave "new emphasis to the requirement that laws restricting religion be neutral and generally applicable." In trying to make the best of *Smith*, he contended that even under *Smith* a law is unconstitutional if it *directly* targets religion.

Smith also suggested that the permissibility of regulated acts depends on the actor's motives, including religious beliefs. Therefore, Laycock maintained, "a law is invalid if it overtly discriminates against religion, if it is enacted for anti-religious motives, if it exempts secular conduct but not religious conduct, if it treats religious reasons for acting less favorably than secular reasons for acting, or if its dominant effect (and not merely an incidental effect) is to suppress religious exercise."

Hialeah's ordinances were neither neutral nor generally applicable. Judge Spellman had found them to be "prompted by the Church's public announcement that it intended to come out into the open and practice its religious rituals," and he had found that "the council's intent was to stop animal sacrifice whatever individual, religion or cult it was practiced by." In other words, Judge Spellman had acknowledged that the ordinances were not neutral and generally applicable laws; they specifically targeted a religious practice. Laycock reminded the Court: "Animals may be killed for food or for sport, because they are sick or injured, or merely because they are 'stray,' 'unwanted,' 'undesirable' or 'of no commercial value.' Any resident of Hialeah can kill an unwanted pet in his yard or in his home, so long as he does not do so in a ritual or ceremony." Ritual animal sacrifice — an expressly religious practice — was the only offense Hialeah sought to penalize. The word *sacrifice*, Laycock underscored, was derived from the same Latin root as *sacred* and *sacrament*. Its original and principal meaning remained that of an offering "to a deity." Animal sacrifice is central to Judaism and important to Islam. For example, the Islamic Feast of Sacrifice, *Id-Ul-Adha*, culminates in a pilgrimage to Mecca and is celebrated with animal sacrifices in the homes of Muslims not on the pilgrimage.

Laycock conceded that after *Smith*, religiously neutral laws were immune from strict judicial scrutiny. But he contended that laws that were not neutral still required a compelling governmental interest to justify infringing on religious freedom. Here, the lower courts had misapplied the compelling governmental interest test in three ways. First, neither lower court had required Hialeah to provide a compelling interest in discriminating against Santeria. Second, the lower courts had reduced the compelling interest requirement to merely that of a "rational or legitimate interest" by assuming that public policy or any "exercise of police power" satisfies the compelling interest test. Third, the lower courts had basically reversed the burden of proof. "Under this Court's precedents," argued Laycock, "the City must prove its compelling interest. To do so, the City must prove that serious harms are actually occurring as a result of petitioners' sacrifices." Judge Spellman had "turned this evidentiary requirement on its head, repeatedly requiring the Church to prove that no animal sacrifice would ever cause harm."

In addition to Hialeah's failure to demonstrate compelling governmental interests, its regulations were not the least restrictive means of advancing those interests. The lower courts had held that Hialeah had an interest in protecting animals from cruel and unnecessary killing. But, Laycock countered, to maintain that sacrificed animals are killed "unnecessarily" presumes that Pichardo's and the church's religious practices were "unnecessary."

Judge Spellman had also found that animal sacrifice poses a threat to public health. Admittedly, dead animals harbor germs and may endanger public health. However, he had upheld the ordinances on that ground not because he found "grave abuses" but "because he let the City prohibit religious exercise for reasons that the City does not deem sufficient to justify prohibition of secular conduct." Likewise, with respect to the alleged threats to *santeros'* health from consuming sacrificed animals that had not been inspected by a public authority, there was no evidence that any person had actually become ill. In short, Judge Spellman had erred in equating or confusing incremental risks with compelling governmental interests.

Finally, Laycock argued that although Judge Spellman had held that Hialeah has a compelling interest in prohibiting the slaughter or sacrifice of animals in areas not zoned for slaughterhouses, neither he nor the appellate court had supported that conclusion. In Laycock's words: "Hialeah has not made it a crime to kill animals. Rather,

Hialeah has made it a crime to sacrifice animals to one's God. Whatever the details and minor differences among the ordinances, the fundamental question in this case is whether religious animal sacrifices can be singled out for discriminatory prohibition. This Court's cases are clear; the answer is no."

In his reply brief, Laycock underscored the bottom line: "The City cannot distinguish animal sacrifice from other killings of animals or other disposal of meat scraps. It forbids sacrifice not because it values animal rights over human rights, but because it places no value on petitioners' free exercise of religion. These ordinances are not neutral and generally applicable, and they are not justified by compelling interests. They violate the Free Exercise Clause as interpreted by *Smith*."

By contrast, Garrett countered that the ordinances addressed a widespread and uncontrolled problem. The issue was simply "the specter of thousands, indeed tens of thousands, of animals being killed in homes and in the streets throughout South Florida with the attendant problems of keeping and feeding the animals, and later, disposing of the remains." Not surprisingly, he emphasized Judge Spellman's finding "that between 12,000 and 18,000 animals are sacrificed in initiation rites alone, during a one year period."

"Do we need to await a plague?" he asked rhetorically in asserting that ritual animal sacrifice poses health risks for the public. Under *Smith*, neutral and generally applicable laws do not require strict judicial scrutiny or compelling governmental interests. Garrett thus argued:

> The Hialeah ordinances are such laws. . . . The prohibition on possession of certain animals within the City limits is similarly unassailable. The ordinances' prohibition of animal sacrifice applies, as the district court found, to animal sacrifice whether practiced by individuals, religious groups, non-religious groups, or cults. Therefore, all aspects of the Hialeah Ordinances are neutral, generally applicable and constitutional under *Smith*.

"Fundamentally," though, Garrett contended, "this case rests on the distinction between 'belief' and 'conduct.' There is no question that laws may greatly burden religious conduct." The Court had upheld the outlawing of polygamy, the handling of poisonous snakes in religious services, and the wearing of yarmulkes by Orthodox Jews in the military. This case was no different. The followers of Santeria, as he put it, "may believe whatever they wish but may not kill animals as an offering to their gods." To hold otherwise would, as the Court observed in *Reynolds v. United States*, "make the professed doctrines of religious belief superior to the laws of the land, and in effect permit every citizen to become a law unto himself."

Hialeah need not prohibit the killing of all animals in order to proscribe ritual animal sacrifice, Garrett insisted. That argument could basically be reduced to one that the ordinances were underinclusive. In *Oregon v. Smith*, the Court had not questioned Oregon's law criminalizing the use of peyote or the state's outlawing of products deemed hazardous to society. Furthermore, Hialeah's ordinances did not discriminate against religious beliefs. "All the evidence established," as Judge Spellman had concluded, "that the council members' intent was to stop the practice of animal sacrifice in the City."

Finally, Garrett countered that there was no constitutionally required exemption for ritual animal sacrifice. *Sherbert v. Verner* was inapplicable; it was distinguishable and confined to religious exemptions from the denial of unemployment compensation. In any event, the district and appellate courts had already held that the ordinances advanced the government's interests — interests in regulating the killing and disposal of thousands of animals in homes and public places, minimizing the hazards to public health, and preventing animal cruelty. Hialeah, concluded Garrett, did not "speculate regarding the harms that occur because of community-wide animal sacrifice" but had introduced a "wealth of evidence regarding the harms to these interests created by wide-scale animal sacrifice throughout the community."

———

Such was the war of words in the briefs. Besides their briefs and those of the amici, lawyers for the church and Hialeah submitted over a thousand pages of motions, pretrial stipulations, transcripts, decisions, and lower court orders; the records and transcripts of the appeal in the Eleventh Circuit, bound in sixteen volumes; and an accordion folder of exhibits. Still, Laycock and Garrett were not done. They had one final shot at influencing the justices. It would come during their oral arguments before the Court.

CHAPTER 6

In the Marble Temple

Arriving at the Supreme Court to hear oral arguments on Wednesday, November 4, 1992, Ernesto Pichardo was anxious and nervous. It was his first time in Washington, D.C. There was local and national media coverage of his case, but the limelight and publicity had costs. Both he and his brother had received death threats — threats thought to have come from someone associated with People for the Ethical Treatment of Animals or the Animal Liberation Front, or possibly from a bitter *santero*. In Washington, Pichardo and Duarte had the protection of an FBI agent, Anthony J. Pinizzoto.

When Pichardo and Duarte were escorted by the Court's police officers through the Great Hall leading to the courtroom, Pichardo remembered feeling reassured. Inside, under the great marble columns lining the hall, are marble statues of all the former chief justices. Pichardo noticed them and immediately thought, "this is like an ancestral shrine. I am at home. I am used to talking to people like this."

For most people, the role of oral arguments is vague. Visitors to the Court usually must stand in long lines before they are seated in the courtroom. Then they typically have only three or four minutes to listen, before being ushered out. That is because the courtroom has only about 350 seats for the public, the news media, and members of the Court's bar — attorneys who have been admitted to practice before it. Only by special request may someone hear entire arguments. Although there are reserved seats for the press, cameras are not allowed in the courtroom, and the justices firmly oppose them. At the end of each term, audio recordings of arguments are made available at the National Archives, and since 2000, transcripts have been made immediately available on the Court's web site (www.supremecourtus.gov).

The importance of oral arguments is clear. The justices hold a conference and vote on a case within a day or two after hearing arguments. They focus the minds of the justices and present opportunities for fresh perspectives. The time allotted for oral arguments has grown consistently shorter during the history of the Court. Early in the nineteenth century, unlimited time was allowed. The Court began cutting back on time in 1848, when it permitted only eight hours per case (four for each side). In 1871, time was cut in half, permitting two hours for each side. In 1911, each side got an hour and a half, and in 1925, time was limited to one hour per side. Finally, in 1970, Chief Justice Warren Burger persuaded the justices to limit arguments to thirty minutes per side.

Oral arguments usually take place about four months after a case has been granted. They are heard every two weeks from the first Monday in October until the end of April, on Mondays, Tuesdays, and Wednesdays. This allows attorneys to file briefs on the merits and the justices and their law clerks to research the cases. The major exception is cases granted after February. By then, the Court's calendar has already been filled, so cases are carried over to the next term, as was Pichardo's.

Justices differ in their preparation for oral arguments. Chief Justice Earl Warren, for one, did not find them "highly persuasive," while Justice Felix Frankfurter was notorious for peppering attorneys with questions. Most justices now come prepared with bench memos drafted by their law clerks. These memos identify the central facts and issues and possible questions to be raised in a case. Because of the workload, Justice Antonin Scalia explained: "You have to have done all of the work you think is necessary for that case before you hear the argument." Contrary to his opinion before his appointment to the Court, he no longer thinks of oral arguments as "a dog and pony show." Like other justices, he goes over each case with his clerks before hearing oral arguments. Chief Justice William Rehnquist walks around the Supreme Court building with one of his clerks and discusses cases prior to oral argument sessions.

"When people come to see our arguments," Justice Anthony Kennedy has emphasized, "they often see a dialogue between the justices asking a question and the attorney answering it. And they think of the argument as a series of these dialogues. It isn't that. As [Justice] John

[Paul Stevens] points out, what is happening is the Court is having a conversation with itself through the intermediary of the attorney."

Justices vary in their style and approach to the questioning of attorneys. Consequently, oral arguments have a different tenor, depending on the Court's composition. In the 1970s and early 1980s, very few justices on the Burger Court asked questions. In contrast, every justice on the Rehnquist Court, except for Justice Clarence Thomas, tends to be aggressive in asking questions. Justices Stevens, Scalia, and David Souter are known for their wit in posing hypotheticals. Chief Justice Rehnquist has a wry sense of humor, and Justice Sandra Day O'Connor is usually terse. Justice Kennedy often helps attorneys by asking clarifying questions.

This Is about Religious Discrimination

Promptly at 10:00, the marshal of the Court announced the sitting of the justices with the traditional introduction: "Oyez! Oyez! Oyez! All persons having business before the Honorable, the Supreme Court of the United States, are admonished to draw near and give their attention, for the Court is now sitting. God save the United States, and this Honorable Court."

In order of seniority, the justices filed into the courtroom from behind the curtains in back of the high bench. They took their seats, with the chief justice at the center and the associate justices on alternating sides, based on seniority. A minute later, Chief Justice Rehnquist announced: "We'll hear argument first this morning in Number 91-948, *Church of the Lukumi Babalu Aye, Inc., v. the City of Hialeah*. Mr. Laycock."

Douglas Laycock rose from the table and went to the podium in front of the justices. At the table sat Duarte and Jeanne Baker, who had assisted with the brief. Although he had argued several cases before federal appellate courts, this was his first time before the justices. In such circumstances, attorneys often hold moot courts to practice their delivery. But several weeks before, Laycock had injured his knee while playing with his children and had undergone surgery. After a week in the hospital, he had spent the last few days before oral arguments at home, preparing himself mentally.

"No case is easy when you've lost below," Laycock knew. He had anticipated rigorous questioning from Justice Scalia and probably others. Thus, he had typed on his word processor a list of possible questions and what he termed "sound-bite answers." He had then gone over and over them, polishing his arguments and responses.

The key for Laycock was to get the justices to focus on Hialeah's overt discrimination against a religious minority. Laycock obviously had to deal with *Oregon v. Smith*, as well. Although he disagreed with that ruling, he would argue that even under *Smith*, the city of Hialeah had infringed on the free exercise of religion. The city's ordinances were not generally applicable laws, but instead directly targeted and discriminated against a religion.

Laycock counted four justices in favor of adhering to *Smith*: Justice Scalia, of course; Chief Justice Rehnquist; and Justices Byron White and Stevens. Justice Harry Blackmun had dissented in *Smith*. So had Justices William Brennan and Thurgood Marshall. But they had been replaced by Justices Souter and Thomas. Still, both of them had said during their recent confirmation hearings that they disagreed with *Oregon v. Smith*. They might be inclined to go along with Laycock's argument. Justice O'Connor had concurred with the result in *Smith* but was critical of its treatment of religious freedom. Laycock counted on her to be sympathetic.

Justice Kennedy appeared to be crucial. He might well cast the deciding vote if the justices split five to four. Laycock had reason to think that Justice Kennedy, though voting with the majority in *Smith*, might be sympathetic to his arguments as well. Laycock thought that, as a relatively new justice on the Court, Justice Kennedy "may not have understood fully what he was voting for in *Smith*." In the preceding term, he had delivered the opinion for the Court in *Lee v. Weisman*. There, the justices had split five to four in holding that school-sponsored prayers at graduation ceremonies run afoul of the First Amendment's (dis)establishment clause. Justice Kennedy's vote and the language of his opinion in *Lee v. Weisman* suggested to Laycock a "willingness to recognize reality." Laycock therefore aimed to persuade Justice Kennedy that the reality in this case — the reality in Hialeah — was overt discrimination against an unpopular religious minority.

Because of his surgery, Laycock arrived at the Court wearing a plastic cast and walking with the aid of crutches. He brought only a few notes with him, on the inside of a manila folder. Already unsure about Laycock since he had lost in the Eleventh Circuit, Pichardo thought: "Do we need this dog? Lazarus, here we go again." It was ironic, for the *orisha* Babalu Aye is, after all, St. Lazarus, the patron saint of the sick and ill. And Laycock did not appear firm on his crutches. He nonetheless did a splendid job under difficult circumstances. He was down-to-earth, focused, and quick in responding to questions.

In the time-honored tradition, Laycock began: "Mr. Chief Justice, may it please the Court." He immediately cut to what was at stake: "This is a case about open discrimination against a minority religion. The four ordinances challenged here were enacted in direct response to the church's announcement that it would build a church and practice [ritual animal sacrifice] in public. They were enacted for the express purpose of preventing the central rituals of this faith. That purpose is recited in the preambles to the ordinances and in the accompanying resolutions. The preambles say that the city's . . ."

At that point, Justices White and O'Connor broke in with questions about the relationship between Hialeah's ordinances and Florida's laws on animal cruelty and whether the case was ripe. Had Pichardo and the Church of the Lukumi suffered a personal injury? Did they have standing to sue? Laycock reassured them that only the ordinances, not state laws banning animal cruelty, were at issue. And the matter of standing dropped by the wayside when Justice Souter asked if Laycock's argument was consistent with *Oregon v. Smith*.

Laycock replied: "*Smith* says that religious acts are subject to neutral and generally applicable regulation, but *Smith* also reaffirms the long line of cases that says Government cannot resolve religious controversies. Government cannot decide whether sacrifice is necessary or unnecessary. An element of the offense under the State law is that the killing of the animal be unnecessary. That's also an element under three of the four ordinances. The only way to prove that sacrifice is unnecessary is to prove that Santeria is a false religion. To believers in Santeria, sacrifice is directly commanded by the gods in considerable detail on each occasion when it is required. To prove it unnecessary, you must prove the religion false, and when the prosecutor has to prove a religion false, the prosecutor is engaged in a heresy trial."

That response provoked a witty retort from the author of *Smith*. An irrepressible and acerbic questioner, Justice Scalia leaned forward to say: "Gee, I'm sure there are a lot of statutes, local, State and Federal, that use the term 'unnecessary.' Do you mean whenever somebody says that God tells him it is 'necessary,' that statute is invalid as applied to that person? That can't be right."

"The prohibition has to depend upon something other than the lack of necessity, Justice Scalia," Laycock continued. If Hialeah had a generally applicable prohibition on killing animals, the religious necessity of the practice would be irrelevant under *Smith*, but Hialeah's ordinances were not that, for they permitted the killing of animals for a whole range of reasons that the city considered necessary. Bow and arrow hunting was permissible, as was the extermination of rats and mice. The only killing of animals deemed impermissible and unnecessary was that done for religious purposes.

Chief Justice Rehnquist, whose dry sense of humor often draws laughter, asked straight-faced, "Is there a lot of bow and arrow hunting in the City of Hialeah?"

"Well, there is bow and arrow hunting by citizens of Hialeah who bring their kill, bring the entire carcass back to the city," Laycock replied. "There are farms in the City of Hialeah. There are veterinary offices that kill animals in Hialeah."

Undeterred, the chief justice persisted: "Well, certainly under our cases the city can deal with one perceived evil at a time without having to deal with the whole ball of wax, can't it?"

"I disagree, Mr. Chief Justice," countered Laycock. "When the first step is the First Amendment, they can't deal with that one step at a time. They have to deal with constitutionally protected activities in a generally applicable way. They can distinguish bow hunting from killing surplus pets one step at a time, but they can't say our one and only step is to suppress this religion and distinguish that from all of the secular killings of animals that they permit."

The point was not, Laycock argued, that the city was dealing with one evil at a time. The point was that the only evil Hialeah was dealing with was one central to a religion. Chief Justice Rehnquist agreed but said: "Let's withdraw from that a little bit and just say, supposing the city council sees what they perceive as this evil, or something that they want to regulate. You say it violates the First Amendment, and you say one reason it does is there are lots of other things that they should have embraced, and their response to that is, well, none of those were going on in the City of Hialeah."

"They have not said that none of those things go on . . . ," Laycock started to say, only to be cut off by the chief's quick retort: "No, but I'm giving . . ." Before he could finish, Laycock shot back: "And the record does not show that none of those things go on." To which the chief responded: "I'm giving you a hypothetical."

"Okay," Laycock conceded, "if no other killings of animals are going on in the City of Hialeah, then their solution under *Smith* would be to draft an ordinance that simply says, it is illegal to kill an animal in the City of Hialeah. That would be unfortunate for my clients, but under *Smith*, that would be a neutral and generally applicable law."

This line of argument troubled Justice Scalia. "They can't make any exceptions to it?" he asked incredulously. "Once they make any exception at all, it's no longer a law of general applicability."

"I'm inclined to think they can't make any exceptions," Laycock replied, "but this case doesn't get us anywhere close to that question."

"You mean," a visibly excited Justice Scalia countered, "you couldn't say you may kill animals for food but not for other purposes — not for sport, not for sacrifice, not for anything but food. You couldn't even make that exception."

Laycock could imagine killing an animal in self-defense, but that only led to a rather heated exchange with Justice Scalia, which Chief Justice Rehnquist finally interrupted: "Could the city council require that all slaughter of animals within the city be done in a humane manner and define humane in a way that the result of which was to either prohibit or require the alteration of these sacrifices?"

Laycock reiterated that a city could impose such a requirement, but only in a neutral, across-the-board way. At this point, Justice Kennedy returned to *Oregon v. Smith* and asked for Laycock's view of the governmental neutrality requirement under *Smith*. Was it an end in itself?

"I don't think it's an end in itself," Laycock replied. "I hope that the purpose is to build into the political process some of the protection for religious minorities that the other half of *Smith* says that the courts are not going to be providing on their own."

"Well," Justice Kennedy observed, "we have a neutrality standard that we administer. What is the purpose of that standard?"

The purpose was to bar government from discriminating against or targeting religion, responded Laycock.

Not satisfied with that answer, but tipping his hand in favor of the church, Justice Kennedy said: "Doesn't the Court have a responsibility to prohibit legislatures from acting with hostility toward religion?"

The justice's question apparently caught Laycock off guard, for he responded rather impatiently: "I can't read your minds, but I think the purpose for which you enunciated that requirement is that requiring the legislature to treat an unpopular minority faith as well as it treats the bulk of the population will give a sort of self-enforcing political protection to the religious minority. They cannot suppress sacrifice unless they are willing to suppress food killings, poison in people's yards, exterminators."

Justice Kennedy responded calmly: "I take it the underlying purpose for that is to avoid a regime which is hostile to religion." Agreeing, Laycock finally realized that the justice had been trying to help him make his argument.

The direction of that exchange moved the chief justice to seek clarification about whether the district court had made any finding on the question of discrimination. Laycock tried to make the best of Judge Spellman's ruling. Judge Spellman had found that the intention of the Hialeah city council had been to prevent animal sacrifice, which, Laycock argued, was essentially a finding of discrimination against religious minorities. In short, Laycock turned Judge Spellman's ruling on its head.

That set off Justice Scalia: "Was there a finding that there was an antagonism towards Santeria? Was there any attempt to suppress the religion as such?"

Animal sacrifice was central to the Church of the Lukumi, Laycock argued. "When you suppress the central ritual, I think you suppress the religion."

Nevertheless, Justice Scalia reasoned perversely: "There have been people like, say, the Thugs were a religious group, I believe, and their central ritual was killing other people. Surely that can be suppressed." Of course, responded Laycock, but only under neutral and generally applicable laws against murder. But Scalia objected: "Hialeah says they have a universal, generally applicable law against ritualistic killing of animals." Laycock continued to try to explain that it was not a generally applicable law.

"No," Justice Scalia shot back. "Anybody who wants to have a ritual and — you're quite right, it doesn't happen very often in fraternities, though I imagine it happens now and then. But why isn't that a valid argument, that — they don't care whether you're doing it for religious reasons or not. They really don't care what your reason is."

Standing firm, Laycock responded sarcastically. "If that's a valid argument, you really have repealed the free exercise clause. Any lawyer in the country with that standard of drafting can draft an ordinance to get any church that happens to be at crosswise with the city council."

At that, Justice Souter came to his defense. "In effect you're saying you've got to define the act without reference to the intention of the people who perform the act." Before Laycock could reply, however, Justice Scalia drew him back into an exchange: "You must ban all killing of animals or else no killing of animals because the purpose can't be taken into account, is that what you're saying?" What about killing in self-defense? Laycock started to say that that would be a harder case, but Justice Scalia again cut him off: "I don't think it's close at all." The justice thought that it was obvious that animals could be killed in self-defense.

Agreeing, Laycock hastened to explain: "The argument would be that saving human life by killing an animal in self-defense is a compelling interest, and that that distinguishes that narrow exception from the religious killings of animals, but what they've done here is say, you can kill animals for almost any reason — just because you're tired of taking care of them, that's a good enough reason. That's necessary — but not for religious reasons."

This line of argument appealed to Justice O'Connor. She wanted to know if the lower courts had applied the compelling governmental interest test — a more rigorous test than that applied in *Smith*. The lower courts purported to do so, but Laycock contended that, effectively, they had considered only whether the ordinances had a "rational basis," a lower standard used to uphold regulations. Asked by the justice where he faulted the lower court, Laycock stressed that Hialeah's ordinances had "nothing to do with the pain to the animals or the problem of disposal. There is no effort to insist that the compelling interest be pursued in a neutral or generally applicable way. There is no insistence that the interest be especially important. What all of these interests are incremental reductions in quite general problems that the city manages for secular purposes. We have carcasses lying on the road when pets are killed by cars. The city doesn't ban cars and it doesn't ban pets. It responds to the problem. An incremental reduction in a general problem cannot be obtained at the expense of the First Amendment."

Chief Justice Rehnquist now interrupted to inquire whether the city could distinguish between the accidental killing of pets and the intentional killing of animals. It could, said Laycock, quickly adding, "but the accident-intention distinction doesn't go to the disposal problem." The disposal problem involved only a small fraction of all the animals sacrificed. Hialeah's ordinances swept too broadly in banning all ritual animal sacrifice.

The chief justice nevertheless insisted that the distinction between accidental and intentional killing had a bearing on the disposal problem. Laycock held firm in countering that "most of the people who intentionally sacrifice do not improperly dispose of the animal. The finding is most of the sacrificed animals are eaten."

"Well," snipped the chief, "like so many cases it depends on how you describe your class." Laycock agreed but stayed focused, insisting that Hialeah had defined a class in a discriminatory way.

Justice Scalia then returned to *Oregon v. Smith*: "Is it their failure to preclude broadly enough, is it the under-inclusiveness of it which precludes the finding of a compelling state interest?"

With time running out, Laycock tried to bury that position. The ordinances were underinclusive with a vengeance. "No killings of animals are included except the religious killings of animals, so it's under-inclusive in a sense, but they really have singled out religion for a prohibition that is applied nowhere else." With that, Laycock concluded: "If there are no further questions, I'll reserve my remaining time."

"Very well, Mr. Laycock," said Chief Justice Rehnquist. "Mr. Garrett, we'll hear from you."

It's about Health, Safety, and Welfare

Garrett had been with the case since the first trial. He had won there and in the Eleventh Circuit. He was confident and had a full command of the background of the case. For almost two decades, he had specialized in litigation, so he did not feel the need to prepare in any special way. He remained basically a trial lawyer, given to theatrics and to arguing facts, not constitutional theory. And although he had argued several times before state supreme courts, this was his first time before the Supreme Court.

"Mr. Chief Justice and may it please the Court." Garrett immediately launched into a discussion of the problems prompting the enactment of the ordinances. But Justice Stevens interrupted and asked about the specific problems. Without missing a beat, Garrett pressed the city's perceived need for the ordinances:

> I think that the record should reflect very clearly that Hialeah was responding to the problem of ritualistic sacrifices taking place in the city. What type of problems are we talking about? We're talking about human health hazards. The human health hazard evidence was evidence concerning the fact that when sacrifices take place, that as many as 52 animals in a single day are killed, and they are killed in a private residence in many instances and then they are decapitated, blood is put into pots, the animals are then often times left out in public places if there is a ritual that requires the animal to be left in a public place. There are problems connected with disease. The disease problems were discussed directly at the trial court as being a problem associated with the fact that the killings take place in residences, and as a result of that you have spilled blood, you have animal parts left in and around houses. That is different than the general problem of garbage.

Breaking into his argument, Justice O'Connor wondered whether it would have been possible for the city to approach the problem by adopting regulations specifying how animals may be killed and how to dispose of their carcasses.

"We believe not," Garrett said, and explained:

> We believe that the nature of the animal sacrifice problem begins all the way from the point in which the animals are possessed for the purposes of animal sacrifice, that the evidence at the district court level was that the inhumane treatment to the animals, which is one of the problems that we cite, begins at that point, and that enforcement is almost impossible because the *botanicas* and other

farms that sell these animals, you have a quickly moving problem. Enforcement is very difficult. More importantly, with respect to the possession of the animals during the sacrifice, there is no evidence that you can solve all of the problems in a house, in a private residence, with respect to a quilt work of ordinances designed to regulate everything that goes on in that private residence from the standpoint of how many animals you have in that residence, how many — how they can be killed, what you do with the blood cauldrons, how you have to hold the knife.

Then you have problems associated with the disposal of the animals, and that the religions often times mandate they be left in public places. The point is that with respect to effectively solving the problems, it is our position that, 1) you couldn't solve all the problems with a series of ordinances, and 2) that the nature of the kind of entanglement that you would be getting involved in as a result of passing this patchwork of ordinances would itself cause a constitutionality problem of entanglement with the religion. Finally, the kind of ordinances that would be required to deal with this problem even to begin approaching effectiveness — and we contend the city is not required constitutionally to enact a large number of ordinances which still don't solve the problem. But assuming that you did enact a large number of ordinances, it's our position that they would be back in court saying you've in effect prohibited us from doing what we need to do in our religion, because now you have told us how we have to hold our knives, how we have to kill them, how we have to handle the blood in the particular ceremonies, and how we have to dispose of the animals, and our gods say that's not what we can do, and therefore we would have the same problem. We'd be back here with a different type of argument, but with the same kind of argument that the regulatory framework that we had created effectively precluded them from practicing their religion, and that is the problem that the city was facing.

Garrett's long argument was finally cut into by the chief: "You might have an ordinance that was easier to defend, though, in that situation, if it had been directed more precisely at the results of these proceedings rather than at the proceedings themselves."

Garrett replied that the ordinances did not target religion. They were, in fact, neutral with respect to religion. But before long, Justice Scalia cut him off. Playing the devil's advocate, he said: "You don't address the problems of hunters who kill animals cruelly, or dispose of their carcasses in a manner that you don't approve of or that's unsanitary, but you do pick upon this religious practice."

"Your Honor," Garrett explained, "there are two responses to that: This is not only a religious practice. There is evidence in the record which has not been mentioned that groups engage in this activity — malevolent magic is mentioned by one of their witnesses to describe what existed with respect to a goat that was cut in half and found on Miami Beach. There are also — there's also evidence in the record with respect to the fact that this particular type of practice is engaged in by Satanists, by witchcraft, voodoo, and this Court has never gone so far as to particularly extend protection to those groups."

Justice White then asked gruffly: "Why shouldn't that go to the compelling interest? You could say that these ordinances do target religion, but they [have] a compelling interest."

Garrett agreed. On the one hand, he contended, Hialeah's ordinances met the neutrality standard of *Smith* because they were not underinclusive. On the other hand, regardless of *Smith*, Hialeah had substantial and compelling governmental interests.

However, Justice Stevens had grown impatient and interrupted to ask: "But you let householders who have animals slaughter — there is an exception made for slaughter of a small number, outside of a slaughterhouse, of a small number of pigs and such. Isn't there an exception for that?" Garrett's response that there was no such exception drew a quick retort from the justice, however.

"Supposing somebody had a sick cat," Justice Stevens said in mock seriousness, "that he thought he had to put him out of his misery, is it unlawful in Hialeah to kill your own cat?" Garrett hesitantly answered in the affirmative, but Justice Stevens, acting incredulous and drawing laughter, persisted. "You mean, I couldn't just drown my own cat in the bathtub or something like that?"

"That would certainly be cruel," replied Garrett.

But the justice continued pressing his hypothetical. "But supposing I gave him an injection of something to put him to sleep, then, instead of doing it in the bathtub." That would be permitted, conceded Garrett.

"Let's go back to your reason for not targeting the unsanitary practice rather than targeting the religious practice that you say ultimately leads to it," Justice Souter interjected, temporarily rescuing Garrett. "Why are you likely to be more effective in targeting a religious practice so defined than you are in targeting an unsanitary practice defined as such?"

Unsatisfied by Garrett's response that the city had identified a problem with discarded animal carcasses in public places, Justice Souter stressed the ineffectiveness of the ordinances, since most sacrifices were conducted in private homes. Trying to get around the problem, Garrett pointed out that the ordinances also banned the possession — possession even in private homes — of animals for use in sacrificial rites.

Still unsatisfied, Justice Souter persisted. "Why are you likely to be more effective in preventing the practice within the private house than you are to be in preventing the disposal in a public place?"

"Because," claimed Garrett, "our view is that there are indications of when an animal sacrifice is about to take place in a house. There are large numbers of people, there are animals outside, and it is the view that we would be able to stop that. On the other hand, with respect to the placement of individual animals throughout the community, that doesn't nearly create the level of conduct or problem that would be perceived by the governmental authorities from an enforcement point of view."

Nonetheless, Justice Souter wanted to know whether the district court had made such findings. Garrett responded: "The district court made some very specific findings about how overwhelming the sacrifice process can become in terms of large numbers of animals being sacrificed in one initiation ceremony in a very small house in Hialeah with a 6 × 10 kitchen, and the district court judge marveled how this could all be done in a sanitary condition under circumstances where the animals were cared for properly under circumstances where the killing was . . ."

"But you don't allow that," interrupted Justice Scalia, again playing the devil's advocate. "I mean, you don't allow that no matter how sanitary, no matter how easy it is rendered for you to police it. You can have a licensed slaughterhouse where killing may occur, because I guess it can be inspected and so forth."

It could be inspected and monitored, insisted Garrett. Yet Justice Scalia would not give up. "But if you're talking about sacrificial killing, you don't even allow it to be done at a place — a temple, a church, whatever — where they say, come in and inspect. Do you want to come in and inspect? Do it. You allow it to be done nowhere, no matter how easy it is for you to police, no matter how willing they are to have you inspect it. You just say, no sacrifice." It was an open question, Garrett admitted.

"Does the City of Hialeah allow people in their homes to trap mice and rats?" Justice O'Connor wondered aloud. "And to boil live lobsters and eat them?" In asking that question, the justice brought levity back into the courtroom. Laughter almost drowned out Garrett's feeble reply. "There is clearly a prohibition in the ordinances about the boiling of lobsters, if you read the ordinances as saying, as I think they do — or any other animals, so I don't believe that the lobsters . . ."

Again drawing laughter, Justice O'Connor continued: "You can't boil the lobster? You can't eat lobster? In Hialeah?" Caught off guard, Garrett said: "I think that technically — a technical reading of the ordinance would say that the boiling of lobsters is claused [sic] by, other animals. In your house, I think there is an exception."

"And what's the exception for the mice and rats?" Justice O'Connor tersely shot back. "Where do I find that?" At that point, Jeanne Baker passed Laycock a note: "We've won."

"The exception for the mice and rats," Garrett tried to say, "would be in the State statute with respect to ordinances." Yet Justice O'Connor countered that the case was about Hialeah's ordinances, not the state's statutes. She found no such exceptions. Garrett again attempted to argue that the ordinances did not cover such killings because they were not ritual animal sacrifices.

Justice Kennedy was stirred. "You talked earlier about the slaughterhouse possibility. Suppose there is an area that's zoned for a slaughterhouse and it is a slaughterhouse, can it be used on Saturdays and Sundays for animal sacrifices?" Trying to duck, Garrett replied that there were none in Hialeah. But the justice would not let go: "I have a hypothetical city and a hypothetical slaughterhouse."

"In that situation," responded Garrett, "I believe that there would under the rulings of this Court probably have to be either a Saturday or Sunday available in order to conduct the rituals in those particular slaughterhouses."

But that would be saying, Justice Kennedy reminded him, that sacrificial rites conducted in a slaughterhouse were protected by the First Amendment. Garrett agreed, seemingly unaware that he was boxed into a corner. Is there a First Amendment right to sacrifice animals? Justice Kennedy asked, cutting to the chase. "No," said Garrett, only to draw more laughter in continuing. "I believe that there is a First Amendment right to, in a situation where you have a circumstance where you are allowing some religious practices to occur in a slaughterhouse, that you would have to allow them to occur on a Saturday or a Sunday."

"Well," Justice Kennedy said with some exasperation, "if a church finds a slaughterhouse that is properly zoned and if it follows standards of applicability that are general for the disposal of animals, does it have a constitutional right to engage in its sacrificial services?"

No, reasserted Garrett, "we do not believe that a church would have a right to engage in animal sacrifice under circumstances that you have now described." Why? "Because we believe that the Constitution does not allow all religious practices to be engaged in even if they are central to the religion. The *Reynolds* case made it very clear that even though polygamy was central to the Mormon Church, that laws basically outlawing the polygamists' activities were laws that were constitutional. We would submit that the fact that it is important to a religion, if there is a legitimate governmental purpose to the particular restrictions . . ."

Justice Kennedy again interrupted him: "Then is the legitimate governmental purpose here the prohibition of sacrifice, per se?"

Garrett replied: "We submit that it is. We submit that animal sacrifice is an appropriate category to be specifically focused on by a series of . . ."

Before he could finish, however, Justice Kennedy again stopped him: "And is it a fair reading of these ordinances to find that that policy is implicit in these ordinances?"

"I think it is a fair reading of the ordinances," Garrett responded. "They in effect attempt to preclude animal sacrifice, and they do that in a number of different ways, and I think that is the question that the Court is facing, whether or not the attempt, and in this case a successful attempt to preclude the animal sacrifice as a governmental problem, is one that can be done under the First Amendment, free exercise provision."

"But would you not agree," Justice Kennedy interjected, "that in order for the prohibition to be legitimate, the public values that you assert are being furthered by the prohibition must not be allowed to be compromised through other exceptions to the killing that you allow, because otherwise you would have nothing left but an antagonism towards the religion. You do not like sacrifice to be done. If you have other values — cruelty to animals or public sanitation or whatever else — at least the other exceptions that you make from your general prohibition cannot permit those things to happen."

Still clinging to his line of argument, Garrett maintained that "the question becomes what particular problems the municipality is facing, and if the municipality has to go and deal with the hypothetical problems in the scope of the ordinance that are not really facing the community, I don't see why that is constitutionally mandated."

Garrett had failed to rise to Justice Kennedy's question and to the occasion. He remained a trial lawyer, comfortable with arguing facts, not dealing with hypotheticals: "It's clear that animal sacrifice carries with it very specific problems that are not attendant with the other types of exceptions that the petitioners point to. There is no record of evidence that we have any of those particular problems, and I think that it's a question of the classification."

"Mr. Garrett," Justice Stevens now interrupted, "the [district] court found specific harms to the animals. They were cruel in the way they did it and there were some disposal problems and certain other specific problems that they found. [Judge Spellman] also found, as I remember it, there's a lot of varieties of this religion. Some have more of some customs and some have slightly different customs. Supposing there was one branch of the religion that required as a part of the ceremony that it be conducted in a slaughterhouse as Justice Kennedy suggests, that it dispose of the remains in a lawful manner, and that it had none of the side effects that trouble you, and very properly. But you have a religion that does sacrifice animals. Now, that religion would be prohibited by your ordinance even if none of the side effects occurred, or were permitted to occur by the religion, is that not correct?"

"That's correct. That would be an incidental impact of the ordinance, and we believe that that would be constitutional under *Smith*," Garrett responded, only to be cut off again by Justice Stevens. Drawing still more laughter, the justice observed: "The other thing that puzzles me, on the one hand you say there are tens of thousands of these sacrifices going on regularly and that's what prompted the ordinance, and then you say, as one very dramatic example of a goat being found on the beach that was apparently very unattractive and unhealthful. . . . But if that happens only once when there are thousands and thousands of sacrifices, which way does the example cut?"

Garrett stumbled, caught off guard by the examples, prompting more questions from Justice Stevens and more laughter in the courtroom over why littering statutes were not sufficient to address the problem of discarded animal carcasses.

There were such statutes, conceded Garrett, but they were ineffective. "They were obviously not accomplishing the purpose for which they were enacted, because it's very difficult to police a situation where people go out at night time or early in the morning with whole animals and leave them in parks, leave them under palm trees as it's dictated under the religious tenets, leave them at railroad crossings, leave them at the steps of courthouses in some instances — all of these dispersal of animal problems are problems that are in the record, and they are not simply a single goat."

"But an easier way to police them," observed Justice Souter, "would be to go back to the example that Justice Kennedy was working you towards to provide some regulated place like a slaughterhouse in which the — kind of the core practice could occur, and yet you reject that."

Garrett, at first, granted that such might be permitted, but when pushed to agree that animal sacrifices in slaughterhouses might also be permitted, he drew the line:

It is our position that that is constitutional. Your Honors, the circumstance that the City of Hialeah was facing was a very specific circumstance — animal sacrifice, inhumane treatment to animals. I would point out that when we talk about putting this activity into a slaughterhouse we are not solving the claim of petitioners that they are entitled to practice their religion as they wish, and the reason why we are not solving that problem is because we never got to the manner in which the sacrifices occur. This is not ritualistic slaughter as it occurs in kosher slaughter, for example. This is an indifferent type of killing. The district court judge was able to conclude that this was an inhumane type of killing because he understood that in — for example, with respect to a four-legged animal an individual hoists it, puts it on a table or altar, attempts to hold it down with one hand, raises a knife in the right hand and attempts in a jabbing motion to cut the carotid arteries in an unreliable method of killing.

A few more quick questions exhausted his remaining minutes, and Chief Justice Rehnquist stated blandly, "Thank you, Mr. Garrett."

A Last Rebuttal

Laycock had only four minutes for rebuttal, but Justice Scalia immediately cut in. "Do you agree, Mr. Laycock, that the limited slaughter that is allowed can only be allowed in a slaughterhouse?"

"That is not correct," countered Laycock:

It can only be allowed where properly zoned. The city attorney, Mr. Gross, testified that on the farms in Hialeah animals are slaughtered under the limited slaughter exceptions in the ordinances. I think it is the case that commercial slaughter is not going on in residential or nonfarm neighborhoods. With respect to the alleged uniqueness of the problem, Mr. Garrett summarized the testimony of the city's expert witness, Mr. Livingstone, about disease factors and the like, but remember, Mr. Livingstone said repeatedly, I'm not talking about animal sacrifice at all, I'm talking about organic garbage. He said it is no different, and the sources of supply of organic garbage are much greater from all of the secular food consumption in the city than they are from these sacrifices.

Now, my clients have always been willing to accept regulation of the farms and *botanicas* which are not protected by the First Amendment. They're willing to accept reasonable zoning on the church itself. They are not willing to give up the rights of their members to sacrifice on special occasions such as births and weddings in the homes, but the church itself can be reasonably zoned, they're willing to comply with disposal regulations, but none of that would satisfy the city.

"How about humane slaughter regulations?" asked Chief Justice Rehnquist, prompting Laycock to respond: "We believe that we are in compliance with humane slaughter. There is a neutral prohibition on torture and torment that is not challenged."

"Why not?" interjected Justice Scalia. "Why not? Why shouldn't you be able to slaughter any way you want — humane or inhumane? If the theory of your case is correct, why — you know, why not go all the way?"

"Well," Laycock said, obviously exasperated, "because we're not tormenting and we're not torturing, we don't have to go all the way. I may be back some year with a different client who does." After the laughter died down, he continued: "The testimony is the method of sacrifice is very quick, except when it fails. The trial judge said it is somewhat unreliable and therefore it is cruel. There is no finding of how often it is unreliable, how often it misses. Those who are experienced in the method said they believe they don't miss, but the intended method of sacrifice is not cruel."

However, Chief Justice Rehnquist wondered: "If the intended method is not cruel, could not the city take into account that the intention just wasn't fulfilled sometimes and it turned out to be cruel in fact?"

"Perhaps they could take that into account in a neutral and generally applicable way," granted Laycock, "but again, look at all the other methods of killing which they permit with no regulation whatever, with no claim that they might be — that they have to be always instantaneous and never a mistake. No human activity has never been a mistake. I can put poison out in my yard in Hialeah and they don't tell me what kind. They don't say it has to be a quick-acting poison. The animal can wander off and suffer for a week, and that's okay with the city. That's expressly authorized in ordinance 87-40. It's only the religion that has to be perfect if it is to exist at all inside the city."

———

Before Laycock could conclude, time ran out at 11:01. Chief Justice Rehnquist thanked him, and the justices turned to the next case. Laycock, Garrett, and their clients went outside and talked with reporters. They could only speculate about the outcome. Usually, the Court does not announce its decision for three to four months after hearing oral arguments. But the Court's decision would not come down for another six months. In the meantime, outside on the steps of the Supreme Court building, Steven McFarland of the Christian Legal Society told reporters: "Anyone in Florida can kill an animal for sport, food, convenience or profit, but not for an exercise of religious worship. This discrimination against religion threatens every believer." Sam Rabinove, legal director of the American Jewish Committee, agreed. A ruling in favor of Hialeah would be "perilous for Jews. States could pass laws regulating kosher slaughter and prohibiting circumcision except when performed by a licensed physician. I'm not saying this will happen, but we would have no protection."

CHAPTER 7

A Thunderbolt

On Friday, June 11, 1993, the Court's ruling came down. The justices had clearly been preoccupied with working out the contours of the First Amendment's religion clauses. The week before, *Lamb's Chapel v. Center Moriches Union Free School District* had been handed down. There, the justices unanimously held that public schools may not deny religious groups, while allowing other groups, the use of school facilities for after-school meetings. A week later, *Zobrest v. Catalina Foothills School District* would come down. In a bitter five-to-four decision, the Rehnquist Court ruled that the (dis)establishment clause does not bar public funding for a sign-language interpreter for a deaf student attending a religious school rather than a local public school. Although often splitting over where and how to draw the line separating government and religion, the justices appeared to be firmly committed to the principle that government may not overtly discriminate against particular religions or religious viewpoints.

At the center of the bench, Chief Justice Rehnquist turned to Justice Kennedy to announce the decision. In accord with the Court's practice, he simply summarized the ruling instead of reading the opinion for the Court. Hialeah had run afoul of the First Amendment. All four ordinances were unconstitutional. There were no dissents. However, a crucial part of Justice's Kennedy's opinion commanded only a plurality, and there were three concurring opinions.

Justice Kennedy Delivers the Opinion of the Court

Chief Justice Rehnquist assigned Justice Kennedy to write the opinion for the Court after a brief discussion and vote on the case at the Friday conference following oral arguments. If the chief had been in the minority, the senior associate justice would have written or assigned the opinion. All the justices, however, agreed that Hialeah had overtly discriminated against the church. Still, there remained sharp disagreements. Justices Blackmun, O'Connor, and Souter did not deem the ruling in *Oregon v. Smith* applicable and considered its analysis misguided. They wanted to reconsider that decision and reestablish broader protection for religious freedom, as under *Sherbert v. Verner.* Justice Scalia, of course, held firm. He and the chief justice were the least inclined to make exceptions for religious minorities and certainly did not want a broad ruling. Justice Kennedy appeared to be in the middle and thus was assigned to write the opinion, relying on *Oregon v. Smith* but without provoking angry dissents from Justices Blackmun, O'Connor, and Souter or from Justice Scalia.

Justice Kennedy divided his opinion into four parts with subdivisions. This was necessary because, although the justices were unanimous on the holding, they were otherwise fragmented on the underlying reasoning for the decision, as the concurring opinions made clear. In the last half of the twentieth century, the justices increasingly put the expression of their individual views above achieving consensus on an institutional opinion. As a result, the number of concurring opinions — opinions agreeing with the result but disagreeing with the Court's reasoning — and dissenting opinions — opinions rejecting both the result and the reasoning — has proliferated. Another trend has been more plurality opinions — opinions that do not command the support of even a majority of the Court. Here, part of Justice Kennedy's opinion, concluding that Hialeah's city council had purposively discriminated against followers of Santeria, failed to command a majority. Only a plurality agreed with that.

A two-paragraph introduction stated the Court's bottom line: "Our review confirms that the laws in question were enacted by officials who did not understand, failed to perceive, or chose to ignore the fact that their official actions violated the Nation's essential commitment to religious freedom. The challenged laws had an impermissible object; and in all events the principle of general applicability was violated because the secular ends asserted in defense of the laws were pursued only with respect to conduct motivated by religious beliefs. We invalidate the challenged enactments and reverse the judgment of the Court of Appeals."

In Part I, Justice Kennedy briefly reviewed the history of Santeria, the enactment of Hialeah's ordinances, and the decisions of the lower federal courts. All the justices agreed to this part. He ran into trouble, though, with Part II A, discussing the requirement of governmental neutrality with respect to religion. He had more success in holding on to a majority in section B, dealing with the application of *Oregon v. Smith*'s requirement for generally applicable laws. Justice Souter declined to join any of Part II. Justice White declined to join section A, while the chief justice and Justices Scalia and Thomas refused to join subsection (2) of Part II A. Only Justices Stevens, Blackmun, and O'Connor joined Justice Kennedy's analysis concluding that the city council had intentionally discriminated against the church.

At the outset of Part II, Justice Kennedy noted that Hialeah did not deny either that Santeria is a religion or that Pichardo and the church were sincere in sacrificing animals for religious reasons. Although animal sacrifice was "abhorrent to some," it had a long historical association with Judaism, Islam, and early Christianity. Quoting from *Thomas v. Review Board of Indiana*, he underscored that "religious beliefs need not be acceptable, logical, consistent, or comprehensible to others in order to merit First Amendment protection."

Turning to the First Amendment's guarantee of the free exercise of religion, Justice Kennedy relied on *Oregon v. Smith* instead of distinguishing or discarding that ruling, as a number of the amicus briefs in support of the church had urged and as Justices Blackmun, O'Connor, and Souter would have done. Accordingly, he ruled that a neutral and generally applicable law need not be justified by a compelling governmental interest, even if it incidentally burdens a particular religious practice. "Neutrality and general applicability are interrelated, and," he observed, "failure to satisfy one requirement is a likely indication that the other has not been satisfied. A law failing to satisfy these requirements must be justified by a compelling governmental interest and must be narrowly tailored to advance that interest. These ordinances fail to satisfy the *Smith* requirements."

Smith's twin requirements of neutrality and general applicability were dealt with in sections A and B of Part II, respectively. At a minimum, the First Amendment required governmental neutrality in the sense that laws may not overtly discriminate against religious beliefs. "Although a law targeting religious beliefs as such is never permissible," Justice Kennedy notably added, "if the object of a law is to infringe upon or restrict practices because of their religious motivation, the law is not neutral, and it is invalid unless it is justified by a compelling interest and is narrowly tailored to advance that interest."

There are a number of ways to determine whether laws are aimed at suppressing a religion. At the very least, they may not discriminate on their face. Justice Kennedy agreed with the church's attorneys that Hialeah's use of the words *sacrifice* and *ritual* in its ordinances was inconsistent with facial neutrality because of their strong religious connotations. Surprisingly, though, he did not deem that conclusive. Even though those words have religious origins, they also have secular uses and meanings. In his view, the ordinances defined *sacrifice* in secular terms, without reference to religious practices.

However, Justice Kennedy did not deem facial neutrality to end the Court's inquiry, as Garrett claimed. "Official action," in his words, "that targets religious conduct for distinctive treatment cannot be shielded by mere compliance with the requirement of facial neutrality. The Free Exercise Clause protects against governmental hostility which is masked as well as overt."

For Justice Kennedy, the combined language and legislative history of the ordinances established their failure of the neutrality test, compelling the conclusion that the suppression of a central element of Santeria was the aim of the ordinances. Although the use of the words *sacrifice* and *ritual* was not conclusive per se, their use supported that conclusion. Resolution 87-66 explicitly stated that the "residents and citizens of the City of Hialeah have expressed their concern that certain religions may propose to engage in practices which are inconsistent with public morals, peace or safety," and it reiterated the city's commitment to prohibit "any and all [such] acts of any and all religious groups." Based on the record of the enactment of the ordinances, the city council had indisputably targeted Santeria.

In addition, the effect or operation of the ordinances impermissibly discriminated against followers of Santeria. As Justice Kennedy put it: "It is a necessary conclusion that almost the only conduct subject to Ordinances 87-40, 87-52, and 87-71 is the religious exercise of Santeria church members."

Ordinance 87-40 incorporated Florida's animal cruelty statute. On its face, it broadly punished "whoever . . . unnecessarily . . . kills any animal." Garrett, of course, defended this ordinance as the epitome of a neutral and generally applicable prohibition. But what remained problematic was how the state statute and Hialeah's ordinance were interpreted by state and local officials. The killing of animals for religious purposes, unless in a licensed slaughterhouse, was basically the only kind of killing deemed "unnecessary." Hunting and fishing, the slaughter of animals for food, the eradication of pests, and euthanasia were all considered necessary killings. Florida officials had even determined that the use of live rabbits to train greyhounds was not an unnecessary killing of animals and was therefore permissible under the state's animal cruelty law, over the protests of animal rights supporters.

Consequently, the ordinance required the government to evaluate particular justifications for the killing of animals. As such, it created a system, in the words of *Oregon v. Smith*, of "individualized governmental assessment of the reasons for the relevant conduct." And even under *Smith*, the government "may not refuse to extend that system to cases of 'religious hardship' without compelling reason." Accordingly, Justice Kennedy found that "the ordinance's test of necessity devalues religious reasons for killing by judging them to be of lesser import than nonreligious reasons," thereby singling out a religious practice for discriminatory treatment.

Likewise, Ordinance 87-52 prohibited the "possession, sacrifice, or slaughter" of an animal with the "intent to use such animal for food purposes," thereby narrowly targeting Santeria. The prohibition applied if animals were killed in "any type of ritual" for the purpose of food consumption. However, the ordinance exempted "any licensed [food] establishment" with respect to "animals which are specifically raised for food purposes" if the activity is permitted by zoning and other laws. The killing of animals by hunters for food consumption or for purposes other than food consumption was not covered, so long as the killing was not part of a ritual. The ordinance also exempted the killing of animals for food consumption during the course of a ritual if it took place in a properly zoned and licensed establishment, such as a kosher slaughterhouse. Hence, the ordinance applied to virtually no one other than *santeros*. Its practical effect was to almost exclusively burden followers of Santeria.

Ordinance 87-71 prohibited the sacrificing of animals but defined *sacrifice* as "to unnecessarily kill . . . an animal in a public or private ritual or ceremony not for the primary purpose of food consumption." That definition excluded almost all killing of animals except for religious sacrifice. Moreover, not even all religious sacrifice was prohibited, because the Jewish practice of kosher slaughtering was exempted.

Finally, the ordinances failed the neutrality test by proscribing more religious conduct than was necessary to achieve the city's interests. The flat ban simply swept too broadly. If Hialeah's interest was the proper disposal of animal carcasses, for instance, the city could enact a general regulation on garbage disposal. During oral arguments, Garrett had claimed that Santeria sacrifices would still be illegal if performed in a licensed slaughterhouse. But the ordinances prohibited Santeria's practice of ritual animal sacrifice even though the city's interest in public health was not thereby threatened. To be sure, Judge Spellman had concluded that a narrower regulation would be unenforceable and ineffective. However, Justice Kennedy found it difficult to understand "how a prohibition of the sacrifices themselves, which occur in private, is enforceable if a ban on improper disposal, which occurs in public, is not."

Similarly, the city could have advanced its interest in preventing animal cruelty by enacting narrower regulations pertaining to the care of animals, regardless of why they are kept. Judge Spellman had concluded that, although the kosher slaughter of animals by severing their carotid arteries was humane, the Santeria practice was "less reliable and therefore not humane." But Justice Kennedy rejected that conclusion. If Hialeah's interest lay in regulating the method of slaughtering animals, it could do so without "a religious classification that is said to bear some general relation to it."

Significantly, Justice Kennedy omitted any mention of Hialeah's interest in preventing psychological harm to children who witness or participate in ritual animal sacrifices.

In subsection 2, Justice Kennedy advanced his view that determining whether a law is neutral under the free exercise clause may be informed by rulings on the Fourteenth Amendment's guarantee of equal protection of the laws. "Here," he reasoned, "as in equal protection cases, we may determine the city council's object from both direct and circumstantial evidence. Relevant evidence includes, among other things, the historical background of the decision under challenge, the specific series of events leading to the enactment or official policy in question, and the legislative or administrative history, including contemporaneous statements made by members of the decision making body. These objective factors bear on the question of discriminatory object."

A review of the legislative history of the ordinances established that they had been enacted "'because of,' not merely 'in spite of,'" their suppression of Santeria. Recalling Garrett's oral arguments, Justice Kennedy emphasized that even though Hialeah had been experiencing significant problems with abandoned animal carcasses, it had not addressed that problem until the week after the Church of the Lukumi announced plans to open to the public. Then, at the city council meeting in June 1987, council members, city officials, and residents had exhibited "significant hostility" toward Santeria. The history of the enactment of the ordinances underscored the aim of the city council "to target animal sacrifice by Santeria worshippers because of its religious motivation."

Section A ended in a single paragraph in subsection 3, concluding: "The ordinances had as their object the suppression of religion. The pattern we have recited discloses animosity to Santeria adherents and their religious practices; the ordinances by their own terms target this religious exercise; the texts of the ordinances were gerrymandered with care to proscribe religious killings of animals but to exclude almost all secular killings; and the ordinances suppress much more religious conduct than is necessary in order to achieve the legitimate ends asserted in their defense. These ordinances are not neutral, and the court below committed clear error in failing to reach this conclusion." Together, the ordinances constituted a pattern of discrimination against the Santeria religion.

Section B turned to *Smith's* second requirement that laws must be generally applicable. A more precise standard was not deemed necessary, because the ordinances fell below that minimum standard for enforcing the First Amendment's guarantee of religious freedom. More specifically, the city's two interests — preventing animal cruelty and promoting public health — were advanced underinclusively. Hialeah's interest in preventing animal cruelty as a justification for its ordinances fell short because they allowed the killing of animals except by means of ritual sacrifice. Fishing and hunting remained legal, along with the extermination of mice and rats, the use of animals in scientific experiments, and euthanasia. The city's contention that such killings were "different," "important," and "obviously justified" was dismissed as ipse dixit.

Likewise, the ordinances were underinclusive in advancing governmental interests in promoting public health and discouraging the consumption of uninspected meat. As Justice Kennedy observed, "The health risks posed by the improper disposal of animal carcasses are the same whether Santeria sacrifice or some nonreligious killing preceded it. The city does not, however, prohibit hunters from bringing their kill to their houses, nor does it regulate disposal after their activity. Despite substantial testimony at trial that the same public health hazards result from improper disposal of garbage by restaurants, restaurants are outside the scope of the ordinances. Improper disposal is a general problem that causes substantial health risks, but which respondent addresses only when it results from religious exercise." So too, the ordinances were underinclusive with respect to discouraging the consumption of uninspected meat. Hunters could still eat their kill and fishermen eat their catch without submitting to governmental inspection.

Ordinance 87-72, prohibiting the slaughter of animals outside of slaughterhouses, was also underinclusive on its face. It exempted "any person, group, or organization" that "slaughters or processes for sale, small numbers of hogs and/or cattle per week in accordance with an exemption provided by state law." Yet the city had failed to justify or reconcile its exemption for businesses slaughtering small numbers of hogs and cattle with its overall goals of preventing animal cruelty and preserving public health.

In Part III, Justice Kennedy underscored that laws discriminating against religious conduct would rarely survive strict scrutiny. All four of Hialeah's ordinances were overly broad or, alternatively, underinclusive in specifically targeting religion without advancing compelling governmental interests.

In a concluding paragraph in Part IV, Justice Kennedy admonished state and local legislators and officials against discriminating against religious minorities. He explicitly reminded the country of the Court's commitment to ensuring governmental neutrality toward religion. Implicitly, the Court was concerned about conserving its limited supervisory capacity, especially in light of its granting review to fewer cases. The justices expected compliance so that they would not have to continue policing governmental infringements on religious freedom. In Justice Kennedy's words:

> The Free Exercise Clause commits government itself to religious tolerance, and upon even slight suspicion that proposals for state intervention stem from animosity to religion or distrust of its practices, all officials must pause to remember their own high duty to the Constitution and to the rights it secures. Those in office must be resolute in resisting importunate demands and must ensure that the sole reasons for imposing the burdens of law and regulation are secular. Legislators may not devise mechanisms, overt or disguised, designed to persecute or oppress a religion or its practices. The laws here in question were enacted contrary to these constitutional principles, and they are void.

Justice Scalia Concurs

In a short concurring opinion joined by the chief justice, Justice Scalia explained his disagreement with Part II of the opinion and his refusal to join subsection 2 of Part II A. Justice Thomas also refused to join that subsection, but neither joined Justice Scalia's opinion nor bothered to explain his position.

Justice Scalia disagreed with Justice Kennedy's analysis of *Oregon v. Smith*'s requirements of neutrality and general applicability as "interrelated, rather than as substantially overlapping." As he put it, "the defect of lack of neutrality applies primarily to those laws that by their terms impose disabilities on the basis of religion; whereas the defect of lack of general applicability applies primarily to those laws which, though neutral in their terms, through their design, construction, or enforcement target the practices of a particular religion for discriminatory treatment." In short, non-neutral laws respecting religious freedom could be generally applicable, precisely because they target particular religions.

Notably, Justice Scalia did not mention that in *Oregon v. Smith* he had cited Judge Spellman's ruling upholding Hialeah's ordinances as an example of neutral and generally applicable prohibitions. He neither offered an explanation for that nor attempted to square that with his vote now to invalidate Hialeah's ordinances.

Justice Scalia's refusal to join subsection 2 was also due to its focus on the motivations—the subjective intent—of Hialeah's city council in enacting the ordinances. Although a staunch defender of analyzing constitutional provisions in light of their "original intent," he remains a champion of the "plain meaning" approach to statutory provisions. Legislative history invites multiple interpretations, as he explained in his book *A Matter of Interpretation: Federal Courts and the Law.* As a result, legislative intent is frequently elusive, if not impossible to determine. In his words, "it is virtually impossible to determine the singular 'motive' of a collective legislative body."

He especially objected to relying on legislative history and intent when applying the free exercise clause. That is because, in his view, the amendment refers only to the effects of laws and makes no reference to the purposes behind their enactment. "Had the Hialeah City Council set out resolutely to suppress the practices of Santeria, but ineptly adopted ordinances that failed to do so," he explained, "I do not see how those laws could be said to 'prohibit the free exercise' of religion. Nor, in my view, does it matter that a legislature consists entirely of the purehearted, if the law it enacts in fact singles out a religious practice for special burdens. Had the ordinances here been passed with no motive on the part of any councilman except the ardent desire to prevent cruelty to animals (as might in fact have been the case), they would nonetheless be invalid."

Justice Souter Concurs

Although not on the high bench when *Oregon v. Smith* came down, Justice Souter sharply disagreed with its holding. He did not deem *Smith* germane to the case at hand and, in any event, thought that *Smith* should be overruled. It was well settled that the free exercise clause bars the government from discriminating against religious beliefs and practices. For him, Hialeah's ordinances were not neutral under any definition. He therefore strenuously objected to continued reliance on *Smith*. *Smith*, to be sure, reaffirmed the principle that "the Free Exercise Clause is offended when prohibiting religious exercise results from a law that is not neutral or generally applicable," and that principle was at issue here. But no less disturbing for him was *Smith's* narrowing of the scope of the free exercise clause.

Smith remained troubling because it introduced a narrow conception of governmental neutrality. Under *Smith*, a law must be neutral with respect to religion in its purpose and on its face. Yet that did not go far enough for Justice Souter. A neutral and generally applicable law in that sense may still burden religious freedom by forbidding something that a religion requires or requiring something that a religion forbids. For example, a neutral, generally applicable prohibition on the consumption of alcohol—a prohibition neutral toward religion and advancing the secular purpose of promoting health—would seriously burden followers of faiths requiring the use of wine in services but not those of other religions or nonbelievers. For Justice Souter, such a prohibition fails the test of governmental neutrality toward religion.

Justice Souter thus drew a distinction between "formal neutrality" and "substantive neutrality." *Smith* embraced only formal neutrality, barring laws that overtly discriminated against religion. By contrast, substantive neutrality requires, along with a secular governmental purpose, that religious practices be exempt from formally neutral laws. As Souter explained: "If the Free Exercise Clause secures only protection against deliberate discrimination, a formal requirement will exhaust the Clause's neutrality command; if the Free Exercise Clause, rather, safeguards a right to engage in religious activity free from unnecessary governmental interference, the Clause requires substantive, as well as formal, neutrality."

Justice Souter also emphasized that in *Smith*, four justices—Justice O'Connor in her concurrence and dissenting Justices Brennan, Marshall, and Blackmun—had rejected the *Smith* rule and embraced what he termed substantive neutrality. He thus raised the ante for overruling *Smith* by implicitly noting Chief Justice Rehnquist's long-standing position that precedents dealing with civil liberties and decided by a five-to-four vote should always be open for reconsideration.

Provoked by Justice Kennedy's reliance on *Smith*, Justice Souter underscored that *Smith* did not expressly overrule prior rulings such as *Sherbert v. Verner* and *Wisconsin v. Yoder*, which recognized religious exemptions from otherwise generally applicable laws. As a result, he emphasized, "we are left with a free-exercise jurisprudence in tension with itself, a tension that should be addressed, and that may legitimately be addressed, by reexamining the *Smith* rule in the next case that would turn on its application."

Reviewing precedents such as *Reynolds, Cantwell, Barnette,* and *Yoder,* which Justice Scalia had distinguished in *Smith,* Justice Souter highlighted the tension between those prior rulings and *Smith* and raised the question of which constitutional rule should be followed. Because *Smith* did not overrule prior free exercise cases, it created for Justice Souter "an intolerable tension in free-exercise law." If there were any doubt about his challenge to Justice Scalia and to *Oregon v. Smith,* Justice Souter underscored that neither *Smith* nor any other recent decision had reexamined the original intent of the free exercise clause. That was another reason to reexamine *Smith.*

Justice Souter concluded by highlighting the importance of religious freedom and the need for the Court to resolve the tension that *Oregon v. Smith* had introduced into the jurisprudence of the free exercise clause. In the tradition of dissenters, he appealed to the wisdom of some future Court:

> The extent to which the Free Exercise Clause requires government to refrain from impeding religious exercise defines nothing less than the respective relationships in our constitutional democracy of the individual to government and to God. "Neutral, generally applicable" laws, drafted as they are from the perspective of the nonadherent, have the unavoidable potential of putting the believer to a choice between God and government. Our cases now present competing answers to the question when government, while pursuing secular ends, may compel disobedience to what one believes religion commands. The case before us is rightly decided without resolving the existing tension, which remains for another day when it may be squarely faced.

———

Justice Blackmun Concurs

In another concurring opinion that reads more like a dissent, which Justice O'Connor joined, Justice Blackmun reasserted his position that the scope of the free exercise clause extends beyond situations in which the government targets a particular religion with discriminatory legislation. Quoting from his dissent in *Oregon v. Smith*, he underscored that burdens on the free exercise of religion "may stand only if the law in general, and the State's refusal to allow a religious exemption in particular, are justified by a compelling interest that cannot be served by less restrictive means."

Justice Kennedy's opinion applied the *Smith* rule, but Justice Blackmun would have reached the same result by applying a different test. Since *Smith* had been wrongly decided, in his view, he maintained that it should be overruled "because it ignored the value of religious freedom as an affirmative individual liberty and treated the Free Exercise Clause as no more than an antidiscrimination principle." Unlike the majority's holding, Justice Blackmun would have expressly applied the strict scrutiny test, under which there could be no question that any regulation targeting religion is ipso facto unconstitutional.

For Justices Blackmun and O'Connor, whenever legislation burdens religious freedom — whether intentionally or unintentionally — the government must demonstrate "that it is the least restrictive means of achieving some compelling state interest." Like Justice Souter, they would have resurrected *Sherbert v. Verner*, which *Oregon v. Smith* had dislodged.

A Remarkable Ruling

On learning of the Court's ruling, Pichardo was jubilant. "Shango," the *orisha* of thunder and lightning, "was on our side. We are amazed by the decision. As an immigrant, as a Cuban, I feel a great honor." At a news conference held at his home, he told reporters: "This is why we came to the United States, because we have freedom of speech and freedom of religion. The Court's decision is of profound significance. Animal sacrifice is an integral part of our faith. It is like our holy meal. The decision means that our people will no longer feel they are outlaws because of the way they worship God."

Douglas Laycock's reaction to the decision was more measured. He pointed out that the conflict boiled down to a "black-white thing," overt discrimination against poor black Cubans who are more likely to practice Santeria than white, middle-class Cubans. And he cautioned that the ruling "only picks up the most obvious cases of suppression. More clever city councils might still enact laws on other matters that would be harmful to religious minorities while staying within the boundaries of the Court's ruling on ritual animal sacrifice."

Other supporters of religious freedom were more upbeat. "An important win for religious liberty," said Forest Montgomery, counsel for the National Association of Evangelicals. "It's a clear message to government officials that they can't single out a church for discriminatory legislation."

"In effect it was permissible to kill an animal for any reason in the city of Hialeah except a religious reason," explained Oliver Thomas, general counsel for the Baptist Joint Committee, who had helped write an amicus brief in support of the church. "That sort of religious gerrymandering has no place in a society committed to freedom of conscience." Thomas conceded, "Many of the groups [joining the brief in support of the church] think animal sacrifice is abhorrent. Certainly none of us take the position that it is proper theologically. But that is not the business of the government to decide — whether a particular practice is proper theologically."

Most followers of Santeria welcomed the ruling and were reassured. Admittedly, some still did not like the attention the lawsuit had focused on their religion. Yet Enoelia Martinez, the owner of a *botanica* located down the street from the Church of the Lukumi's first site in Hialeah, said: "This is very good for me. In reality, there has been a lot of pressure on people who just want to practice their religion. Now, I can go back to giving spiritual consultations." Irma Gonzalez, the owner of another *botanica* in Hialeah, agreed. "Ellegua is hungry," she said. "He needs to be fed his roosters to strengthen him." A number of animal cruelty cases against *santeros* across the country were also dismissed in light of the Court's decision.

Not surprisingly, animal rights advocates denounced the ruling. "An obscene, bizarre and disastrous mistake" was how Roger Caras, president of the American Society for the Prevention of Cruelty to Animals, put it. "This voodoo-like religion is not legitimate in the context of modern America." Likewise, the ASPCA's chief law enforcement officer, Herman Cohen, warned that even animal cruelty laws might now be called in to question. "Until today," he told reporters, "taking an animal into a living room, cutting its throat and saying a prayer was prohibited. I don't know if that's true anymore." Santeria's ritual animal sacrifice "is pretty vicious," charged Amy Bertsch of the People for the Ethical Treatment of Animals. "This is not an issue of religious rights," maintained Nancy Alexander of Florida's Animal Rights Foundation. "They can practice whatever they want, but this is an issue of animal cruelty." Marc Paulhus, head of Florida's chapter of the Humane Society of the United States, told Peter Jennings on ABC's *World News Tonight:* "We're totally stunned and, indeed, we are angry about this ruling. What it means is that tens of thousands of animals can now be legally sacrificed on the altar of religious freedom."

For his part, Hialeah's Mayor Raul Martinez was resigned to the decision. He estimated that the lawsuit had cost the city about $350,000 in legal fees. "That's a huge chunk of change that could have repaired a lot of streets and served a lot of hot breakfasts to children," he lamented. He told reporters that the city would not enact further legislation on the matter. "I don't think the city of Hialeah can stand another bill this big," he said. But in response to the suggestion that *santeros* who own *botanicas* should, in light of the Court's ruling, receive a religious exemption from the city's licensing fees for retailers, Martinez drew the line. "Every business has to pay for a license, and a *botanica* is a place of business, like a drugstore. It is not a place of worship, like a church. They are mixing apples and oranges here."

———

The ruling was remarkable in many ways. The Court reached down to protect the religious freedom of a little-understood and unpopular minority. The justices, as Pichardo had predicted, saw through the local politics in Hialeah to the discrimination of Cuban immigrants turning against each other. The Rehnquist Court brought the "outliers" in South Florida into conformity with the national principle that government may not overtly discriminate against religious minorities. To be sure, the Court relied on, rather than overruled, *Oregon v. Smith.* Still, the Rehnquist Court, one of the most conservative Courts since the early twentieth century, vindicated the principle of governmental neutrality toward the free exercise of religion.

The ruling was no less remarkable for the fact that the Court granted review in the first place and did not later dismiss it as improvidently granted. Neither Pichardo nor any other follower of Santeria had been fined or arrested under Hialeah's ordinances. Yet no one on the Court appeared to be worried about such traditional concerns as standing to sue.

In this and other rulings, conservative and liberal justices alike no longer seem to be concerned about their "gatekeeping" function or defending what was once called the "passive virtues" of judicial review. Even conservative justices are no longer animated by concerns about "judicial activism" that once preoccupied traditional advocates of judicial self-restraint such as Justice Frankfurter. Both liberal and conservative justices, though disagreeing about how to apply constitutional principles, take for granted the Court's institutional role as the country's umpire in superintending and actively challenging democratically elected majorities.

Ernesto Pichardo and the Church of the Lukumi won a major victory for religious freedom. In the six years of litigation, much changed, but much also remained the same. Shortly after the Court's decision, *iyalosha* Carmen Pla told a reporter: "We have our own beliefs and relationship with our gods, and that is all very private." In fact, in December 1992, prior to the Court's ruling, *babalawos* affiliated with the Church of the Lukumi voted not to perform ritual animal sacrifice in public. Santeria continued to flourish in South Florida and elsewhere, but largely in private, in the homes of *santeros* and in *botanicas*.

————

Ironically, two weeks after the Court's decision, Pichardo became embroiled in another controversy over animal sacrifice. A supporter in his fight against Hialeah's ordinances, Rigoberto Zamora, announced that he would publicly perform an animal sacrifice. Zamora even invited reporters and television crews to cover the ceremony. Pichardo urged him not to do so, saying that it "would be viewed as offensive to our religious traditions, as well as the general community." Pichardo also now explained to reporters: "Public offering of animals is offensive to our traditions and violates the privacy of the ritual."

On June 26, 1993, Zamora performed the rite nonetheless. Outside of his apartment in Miami Beach, about forty demonstrators from People for the Ethical Treatment of Animals protested. They shouted repeatedly: "Stop the torture, stop the pain, Santeria is insane! Stop the torture, stop the pain, Santeria is insane!"

Inside the apartment, with cameras rolling, Zamora sacrificed fifteen animals: a black ram, three goats, five chickens, two roosters, two pigeons, and two guinea hens. "What before we had to hide, now we can do in the open," he said, after pouring the ram's blood over an altar dedicated to Shango. "We feel different now — but we have always done this, legal or not."

Zamora said that he "wanted to demonstrate that we kill animals quickly. I wanted to prove to the whole country we're not cruel to animals. We're a religion, just like any other." But the two-hour ceremony did not go well. He had trouble severing the neck of a goat with a dull steak knife and had to switch to a sharper knife. Zamora then killed one of the guinea hens by slamming it against the floor, before cutting off its head. Later, he ripped the head off a pigeon with his hands.

The outrage of animal rights advocates spread to *santeros* and created an uproar in South Florida. Within days, the publicity forced Zamora to concede: "It was an error on my part. It had a different effect than the one I was anticipating." Most people, he now realized, "just saw an animal being killed and they're used to buying their meats in a supermarket."

Pichardo rejected Zamora's expression of regret. He organized a group of about 300 *santeros* to sign a petition condemning Zamora and calling for his ouster from the Santeria priesthood. Zamora vowed never again to sacrifice an animal in public. But he rejected the idea that Pichardo or any other *santero* had the authority to sanction him.

The controversy quickly ended their friendship. "Zamora is a charlatan," Pichardo told reporters. "*Babalawos* who have spoken with him, questioned him, say he is a complete imposter. We have been told by representatives of the religion in Cuba that Zamora was never initiated. Even his family says it isn't so. People get off the plane from Cuba, set up in an apartment somewhere, and claim they are *babalawos*. They cheat people. This is why we need certification, why we need an institution — to weed these people out."

Zamora and a few supporters countered that Pichardo was monopolizing the religion and trying to control it. "Pichardo thinks he is the pope of Santeria," charged Zamora. "He wants to be the Pope, and in Santeria, there is no Pope. All *santeros* are independent. The Supreme Court ruling has gone to his head." Zamora, who heads his own International Union of Yoruba Religion Rights in Little Havana and advertises his services in Spanish-language newspapers in South Florida and the Caribbean, strongly objected to the church's requiring annual dues and certification of *santeros*. Pichardo, he reiterated, "obviously wants to assume the role of owner, director, and founder of the Yoruba religion."

The public feud underscored the racial and class tensions within the Cuban community. Whereas Pichardo is a white immigrant who arrived during the 1960s exodus after Castro's rise to power, Zamora is a black Cuban from the 1980 Mariel boatlift. Fifteen years older than Pichardo, he had been a foot soldier in the army fighting against

Castro's revolution. He deeply resented being called a charlatan. "I was dipped in the river," he recalled. "My head was painted. They put saints on my head. I slept on the floor for seven days. I went to drummings. I can tell you my godmother and godfather and the witnesses."

For Zamora, "the only people who really understand this religion are black people like me. It comes from Africa. It is in my blood. Pichardo is white. It isn't in his blood. The whites are trying to steal our religion because of the money in it. But more than that I was persecuted in this country for practicing my religion. I had to move six or seven times over the years. One time the police came to my apartment in Little Havana, I had blood all over me. I had to hide the carcasses of the animals under a bed. The police told me to open up. I said, 'Only if you have a warrant.' They went away, and the people in the ceremony finally left. Pichardo didn't suffer that, because this society is racist. I have suffered for my religion. And in that religion, power does not come from an institution. It comes from my own power of prophecy, like *santeros* all through the ages. Pichardo is an enemy of the religion. He joined the police in attacking me."

Pichardo viewed the matter very differently. The Mariel boatlift brought many imposters and created an image problem for Santeria by associating it with cocaine dealers and drug trafficking. "Our religion was almost bankrupted by that kind of person," he countered. "The problem we had in the eighties was, we weren't institutionalized. We couldn't police ourselves. The power of divination must be developed through training and study. Certification of priests will assure that. We need to return the religion finally to the institution it was and is in Africa."

The public uproar over the scenes of Zamora's sacrifices eventually led prosecutors to charge him with four counts of animal cruelty for using a dull knife and causing the animals unnecessary suffering. Each count carried a $5,000 fine and a year imprisonment.

Zamora's public defender, Brian Tannebaum, claimed that the charges were politically inspired. "There must have been pressure from an outside group," he told reporters. Indeed, prosecutors waited almost two years before filing the charges in mid-June 1995, just three days before the statute of limitations would have run out.

Ironically, both Pichardo and animal rights advocates would testify against Zamora at his trial. Zamora had very few defenders, but the

ACLU came to his aid. As ACLU attorney Benjamin Waxman explained: "In this case we feel that the animal cruelty statute, which has a legitimate purpose, is clearly being used to get at someone practicing their religion."

Zamora pled not guilty, but just as the trial was about to begin a year later, in June 1996, a plea bargain was reached. Zamora agreed to plead guilty to one charge of animal abuse. In return, Judge Victoria Sigler sentenced him to two years' probation and 400 hours of community service at the Catholic Community Services for the Elderly Center in Miami.

———

Within months of the Court's ruling, Congress enacted the Religious Freedom Restoration Act (RFRA) of 1993. Due to opposition to *Oregon v. Smith*, a coalition of virtually every faith had been lobbying Congress to enact the RFRA and reestablish the pre-*Smith* test for balancing claims of religious minorities laid down in *Sherbert v. Verner*.

Ironically, in spite of the broad coalition supporting the RFRA, and given its own disagreement with *Oregon v. Smith*, the U.S. Catholic Conference delayed enactment of the law for two years. The Catholic Conference and the National Right to Life Committee opposed the RFRA because of their anti-abortion stance. The Catholic Conference was concerned that Jewish women might invoke the RFRA in challenging state laws banning abortion in the event *Roe v. Wade* was overturned. Under Talmudic law, abortion is not a choice but a religious duty when the life of the mother is threatened. The conference's concern appeared to be exaggerated, since no state restricting abortions had failed to make an exception when a woman's health or life is at stake. And in 1992, a bare majority of the Court had reaffirmed the "essence of *Roe v. Wade*" in *Planned Parenthood of Southeastern Pennsylvania v. Casey*. Even if *Roe* were overruled, it remained highly unlikely that courts would hold that the rights of women seeking abortions because childbirth endangered their lives were outweighed by governmental interests in protecting the unborn. Still other opponents of the RFRA argued that Congress lacked the authority to override the Court's interpretation of the First Amendment.

On October 27, 1993, Congress enacted the RAFA. In doing so, it boldly challenged the Court in listing among the purposes of the act:

(1) to restore the compelling interest test as set forth in *Sherbert v. Verner*, 374 U.S. 398 (1963) and *Wisconsin v. Yoder*, 406 U.S. 205 (1972) and to guarantee its application in all cases where free exercise of religion is substantially burdened; and

(2) to provide a claim or defense to persons whose religious exercise is substantially burdened by government.

The RFRA specifically prohibited government at all levels from "substantially burdening" a person's exercise of religion, even if the burden results from a generally applicable law, unless the government demonstrates that the burden "(1) is in furtherance of a compelling governmental interest; and (2) is the least restrictive means of furthering that compelling governmental interest." In resurrecting the test laid down in *Sherbert v. Verner*, Congress purported to override *Oregon v. Smith*.

Subsequently, the constitutionality of the RFRA was challenged in a case involving zoning regulations applied to church property. This time, the case arriving on the Court's doorstep, *City of Boerne v. Flores*, pitted religious freedom against governmental interests in historical preservation. Paradoxically, the RFRA was invoked and defended in the Supreme Court by the Catholic Church.

Situated on a hill in the city of Boerne, Texas, St. Peter the Apostle Church had been built in 1923 in replication of the mission style of the region's earlier history. It could accommodate about 230 worshippers but became too small for the growing number of parishioners attracted to the Reverend Anthony Cummins. Accordingly, the archbishop of San Antonio authorized the expansion of the building. Shortly afterward, the Boerne city council passed an ordinance directing its Historical Landmark Commission to develop a preservation plan for historical landmarks. Under the ordinance, the commission was given the authority to preapprove any construction affecting historic landmarks and buildings. When the archbishop applied for a construction permit, city authorities designated the church a historic landmark and denied the application. The archbishop then filed a lawsuit in federal district court, claiming that the city had violated the church's religious freedom as guaranteed by the RFRA. In defending the city's decision to deny the permit, attorneys countered that enactment of the RFRA had exceeded Congress's power, under Section 5 of the Fourteenth Amendment, to enforce constitutional rights. A federal district court agreed, but the Court of Appeals for the Fifth Circuit reversed, and the city appealed.

When the Supreme Court heard oral arguments in *City of Boerne v. Flores,* Douglas Laycock returned to argue before the justices. This time defending the RFRA, he faced a slightly different lineup of justices, but one that appeared promising. Shortly after *Church of the Lukumi Babalu Aye* came down, Justice White, a 1962 appointee of President John F. Kennedy, retired. For the first time in a quarter of a century, a Democratic president had the opportunity to appoint a member of the Court. President Bill Clinton appointed Ruth Bader Ginsburg to fill the vacancy. Justice Ginsburg was known as a champion of women's rights, "the Thurgood Marshall of the women's movement." In the 1970s, as the lead attorney for the ACLU's Women's Rights Project, she had argued six cases (winning five) before the Court that legitimated the application of the Fourteenth Amendment's equal protection clause to gender discrimination. In 1980, President Jimmy Carter had appointed her to the Court of Appeals for the District of Columbia Circuit. With her elevation in 1993, she became the sixth Jewish and second female justice in the history of the Court.

A year later, Justice Blackmun stepped down, and Clinton named another Jewish justice, Stephen G. Breyer. Breyer, a former Harvard Law School professor, had been a judge on the Court of Appeals for the Second Circuit since 1980. For the first time in the history of the Court, there were more non-Protestants sitting on the bench than Protestants: two Jews — Ginsburg and Breyer — and three Catholics — Scalia, Kennedy, and Thomas.

As he had when arguing the case for the Church of the Lukumi, Laycock faced relentless questioning. This time, though, he did not prevail. The justices split six to three in striking down the RFRA. Again writing for the Court, Justice Kennedy ruled that Congress had exceeded its power under Section 5 of the Fourteenth Amendment. Section 5 empowers Congress to enforce by appropriate legislation the amendment's guarantees of due process and equal protection of the law. Based on the history of the Fourteenth Amendment, Justice Kennedy held that Congress's power is solely "remedial" and "preventive." In other words, Congress has no power to define constitutional rights or to expand their scope beyond that recognized by the

Court. As he observed: "Legislation which alters the meaning of the Free Exercise Clause cannot be said to be enforcing the Clause. Congress does not enforce a constitutional right by changing what the right is. It has been given the power 'to enforce,' not the power to determine what constitutes a constitutional violation."

Clearly, a majority of the Rehnquist Court was indignant about Congress's attempt to override *Oregon v. Smith*. Justice Kennedy also underscored the sweeping nature of the RFRA and its costs for states and localities in accommodating religious minorities, particularly with respect to zoning laws. He dismissed the idea of giving heightened scrutiny to such claims of religious freedom, explaining: "When the exercise of religion has been burdened in an incidental way by a law of general application, it does not follow that the persons affected have been burdened any more than other citizens, let alone burdened because of their religious beliefs."

Justice Stevens issued a concurring opinion maintaining that the act ran afoul of the First Amendment's (dis)establishment clause. In his view, "the Religious Freedom Restoration Act of 1993 (RFRA) is a 'law respecting an establishment of religion' that violates the First Amendment to the Constitution."

Justice Scalia issued a concurring opinion as well, rebutting Justice O'Connor's dissenting opinion and again defending *Oregon v. Smith*. As in *Smith*, he claimed: "To say that a nondiscriminatory religious-practice exemption is permitted, or even that it is desirable, is not to say that it is constitutionally required."

Justice O'Connor's lengthy dissenting opinion was joined by Justices Souter and Breyer. Justice Souter also filed a dissent of his own, reasserting the doubts he had expressed in *Church of the Lukumi* about the precedential value of *Oregon v. Smith*. Justice O'Connor exhaustively reviewed the colonial history and "original intent" of the First Amendment's guarantee of religious freedom to counter Justice Scalia's interpretation in *Smith*. Her dissent appealed to a future Court to reconsider *Smith* by underscoring that "the Religion Clauses of the Constitution represent a profound commitment to religious liberty. Our Nation's Founders conceived of a Republic receptive to voluntary religious expression, not of a secular society in which religious expression is tolerated only when it does not conflict with a generally applicable law. . . . [T]he Free Exercise Clause is properly understood as an affirmative guarantee of the right to participate in religious activities without impermissible governmental interference, even when a believer's conduct is in tension with a law of general application."

———

In a settlement agreement, the city of Hialeah agreed to pay almost half a million dollars for the legal expenses incurred by Ernesto Pichardo and the church. Pichardo and the church did not pursue further legal action to hold the mayor and city council personally liable for violating their First Amendment right to the free exercise of religion. But Hialeah paid one dollar to the church as compensation and as a symbol of their reconciliation.

Years later, Hialeah remains a working-class Hispanic community, though it has changed in some ways. There is greater tolerance of Santeria. "There is less hostility from some Christian denominations, fewer reports of discrimination against practitioners," observed Pichardo, "and people are not as paranoid about seeking priests." Still, the claim that animal sacrifices cause children psychological trauma lingers. It remains a major problem for church members, particularly those involved in divorce and child custody cases in which only one parent practices Santeria. Lawyers often do not want to defend the practice in such cases, and the number of cases continues to grow.

Almost fifteen years after the controversy exploded, the original site of the Church of the Lukumi, the former used-car lot at 173 West Fifth Street, remains vacant. The building has been bulldozed and the lot cleared. The site, on which an apartment building may eventually be built, passes virtually unnoticed by the steady stream of traffic up Okeechobee Road, running between it and the Miami River.

In the neighborhood of small, well-maintained houses and rows of low-income apartments, several *botanicas* remain open for business. They are a short distance from city hall and in close proximity to Baptist, Catholic, and Pentecostal churches. Raul Martinez is still the city's controversial mayor. The problem of discarded animal carcasses no longer appears to loom large for the community, however. "From time to time we find animal carcasses next to palm trees," he said. "We pick it up and discard it, and that's that."

From 1987 to 1999, the Church of the Lukumi Babalu Aye operated out of a storefront on Palm Avenue. Besides offering its services, the church sponsored conferences and other educational programs. *Iyalosha* Pla continued to hold séances. Ernesto and Fernando Pichardo set up a web site for the church. "It's cyberspace Santeria," says Pichardo. He also worked for a while trying to set up an "*Orisha* Depot" that would provide *santeros* with herbs and other ceremonial items at discount prices. But in 1999, the Church of the Lukumi closed its doors because of the annual forecast from the *orishas*. Then in 2000, Ernesto explained, "we were told to reevaluate the concept, disconnect, and begin to measure what is obsolete, what needs to be reshaped, and how to actualize it. In the meantime," he added, "we are growing nationally and internationally." The constantly ringing phone and fax in his home are evidence of the demand for his services.

APPENDIX:
HIALEAH'S RESOLUTIONS AND ORDINANCES ON RITUAL ANIMAL SACRIFICE

CITY OF HIALEAH, FLORIDA, RESOLUTION 87-66
(ADOPTED JUNE 9, 1987)

WHEREAS, residents and citizens of the City of Hialeah have expressed their concern that certain religions may propose to engage in practices which are inconsistent with public morals, peace or safety, and

WHEREAS, the Florida Constitution, Article I, Declaration of Rights, Section 3, Religious Freedom, specifically states that religious freedom shall not justify practices inconsistent with public morals, peace or safety.

NOW, THEREFORE, BE IT RESOLVED BY THE MAYOR AND CITY COUNCIL OF THE CITY OF HIALEAH, FLORIDA, that:

1. The City reiterates its commitment to a prohibition against any and all acts of any and all religious groups which are inconsistent with public morals, peace or safety.

CITY OF HIALEAH, FLORIDA, ORDINANCE 87-40
(ADOPTED JUNE 9, 1987)

WHEREAS, the citizens of the City of Hialeah, Florida, have expressed great concern over the potential for animal sacrifices being conducted in the City of Hialeah; and

WHEREAS, Section 828.27, Florida Statutes, provides that "nothing contained in this section shall prevent any county or municipality from enacting any ordinance relating to animal control or cruelty to animals which is identical to the provisions of this Chapter . . . except as to penalty."

NOW, THEREFORE, BE IT ORDAINED BY THE MAYOR AND CITY COUNCIL OF THE CITY OF HIALEAH, FLORIDA, that:

Section 1. The Mayor and City Council of the City of Hialeah, Florida, hereby adopt Florida Statute, Chapter 828 — "Cruelty to Animals" (copy attached hereto and made a part hereof), in its entirety (relating to animal control or cruelty to animals), except as to penalty.

Section 2. Repeal of Ordinances in Conflict. All ordinances or parts of ordinances in conflict herewith are hereby repealed to the extent of such conflict.

Section 3. Penalties. Any person, firm or corporation convicted of violating the provisions of this ordinance shall be punished by a fine, not exceeding $500.00, or by a jail sentence, not exceeding sixty (60) days, or both, in the discretion of the Court.

Section 4. Inclusion in Code. The provisions of this Ordinance shall be included and incorporated in the Code of the City of Hialeah, as an addition or amendment thereto, and the sections of this Ordinance shall be re-numbered to conform to the uniform numbering system of the Code.

Section 5. Severability Clause. If any phrase, clause, sentence, paragraph or section of this Ordinance shall be declared invalid or unconstitutional by the judgment or decree of a court of competent jurisdiction, such invalidity or unconstitutionality shall not affect any of the remaining phrases, clauses, sentences, paragraphs or sections of this ordinance.

Section 6. Effective Date. This Ordinance shall become effective when passed by the City Council of the City of Hialeah and signed by the Mayor of the City of Hialeah.

CITY OF HIALEAH RESOLUTION 87-90
(ADOPTED AUGUST 11, 1987)

WHEREAS, the residents and citizens of the City of Hialeah, Florida, have expressed great concern regarding the possibility of public ritualistic animal sacrifices in the City of Hialeah, Florida; and

WHEREAS, the City of Hialeah, Florida, has received an opinion from the Attorney General of the State of Florida, concluding that public ritualistic animal sacrifices is [*sic*] a violation of the Florida State Statute on Cruelty to Animals; and

WHEREAS, the Attorney General further held that the sacrificial killing of animals other than for the primary purpose of food consumption is prohibited under state law; and

WHEREAS, the City of Hialeah, Florida, has enacted an ordinance mirroring state law prohibiting cruelty to animals.

NOW, THEREFORE, BE IT RESOLVED BY THE MAYOR AND CITY COUNCIL OF THE CITY OF HIALEAH, FLORIDA, that:

Section 1. It is the policy of the Mayor and City Council of the City of Hialeah, Florida, to oppose the ritual sacrifices of animals within the City of Hialeah, Florida. Any individual or organization that seeks to practice animal sacrifice in violation of state and local law will be prosecuted.

CITY OF HIALEAH, FLORIDA, ORDINANCE 87-52
(ADOPTED SEPTEMBER 8, 1987)

WHEREAS, the residents and citizens of the City of Hialeah, Florida, have expressed great concern regarding the possibility of public ritualistic animal sacrifices within the City of Hialeah, Florida; and

WHEREAS, the City of Hialeah, Florida, has received an opinion from the Attorney General of the State of Florida, concluding that public ritualistic animal sacrifice, other than for the primary purpose of food consumption, is a violation of state law; and

WHEREAS, the City of Hialeah, Florida, has enacted an ordinance (Ordinance No. 87-40), mirroring the state law prohibiting cruelty to animals.

WHEREAS, the City of Hialeah, Florida, now wishes to specifically prohibit the possession of animals for slaughter or sacrifice within the City of Hialeah, Florida.

NOW, THEREFORE, BE IT ORDAINED BY THE MAYOR AND CITY COUNCIL OF THE CITY OF HIALEAH, FLORIDA, that:

Section 1. Chapter 6 of the Code of Ordinances of the City of Hialeah, Florida, is hereby amended by adding thereto two (2) new Sections 6-8 "Definitions" and 6-9 "Prohibition Against Possession of Animals for Slaughter or Sacrifice," which is to read as follows:

Section 6-8. Definitions:

1. Animal — any living dumb creature.

2. Sacrifice — to unnecessarily kill, torment, torture, or mutilate an animal in a public or private ritual or ceremony not for the primary purpose of food consumption.

3. Slaughter — the killing of animals for food.

Section 6-9. Prohibition Against Possession of Animals for Slaughter or Sacrifice:

1. No person shall own, keep or otherwise possess, sacrifice, or slaughter any sheep, goat, pig, cow or the young of such species, poultry, rabbit, dog, cat, or any other animal, intending to use such animal for food purposes.

2. This section is applicable to any group or individual that kills, slaughters or sacrifices animals for any type of ritual, regardless of whether or not the flesh or blood of the animal is to be consumed.

3. Nothing in this ordinance is to be interpreted as prohibiting any licensed establishment from slaughtering for food purposes any animals which are specifically raised for food purposes where such activity is properly zoned and/or permitted under state and local law and under rules promulgated by the Florida Department of Agriculture.

Section 2. Repeal of Ordinance in Conflict. All ordinances or parts of ordinances in conflict herewith are hereby repealed to the extent of such conflict.

Section 3. Penalties. Any person, firm or corporation convicted of violating the provisions of this ordinance shall be punished by a fine, not exceeding $500.00, or by a jail sentence, not exceeding sixty (60) days, or both, in the discretion of the Court.

Section 4. Inclusion in Code. The provisions of this Ordinance shall be included and incorporated in the Code of the City of Hialeah, as an addition or amendment thereto, and the sections of this Ordinance shall be re-numbered to conform to the uniform numbering system of the Code.

Section 5. Severability Clause. If any phrase, clause, sentence, paragraph or section of this Ordinance shall be declared invalid or unconstitutional by the judgment or decree of a court of competent jurisdiction, such invalidity or unconstitutionality shall not affect any of the remaining phrases, clauses, sentences, paragraphs or sections of this ordinance.

Section 6. Effective Date. This Ordinance shall become effective when passed by the City Council of the City of Hialeah and signed by the Mayor of the City of Hialeah.

CITY OF HIALEAH, FLORIDA, ORDINANCE 87-71
(ADOPTED SEPTEMBER 22, 1987)

WHEREAS, the City Council of the City of Hialeah, Florida, has determined that the sacrificing of animals within the city limits is contrary to the public health, safety, welfare and morals of the community; and

WHEREAS, the City Council of the City of Hialeah, Florida, desires to have qualified societies or corporations organized under the laws of the State of Florida, to be authorized to investigate and prosecute any violation(s) of the ordinance herein after set forth, and for the registration of the agents of said societies.

NOW, THEREFORE, BE IT ORDAINED BY THE MAYOR AND CITY COUNCIL OF THE CITY OF HIALEAH, FLORIDA, that:

Section 1. For the purpose of this ordinance, the word sacrifice shall mean: to unnecessarily kill, torment, torture, or mutilate an animal in a public or private ritual or ceremony not for the primary purpose of food consumption.

Section 2. For the purpose of this ordinance, the word animal shall mean: any living dumb creature.

Section 3. It shall be unlawful for any person, persons, corporations or associations to sacrifice any animal within the corporate limits of the City of Hialeah, Florida.

Section 4. All societies or associations for the prevention of cruelty to animals organized under the laws of the State of Florida, seeking to register with the City of Hialeah for purposes of investigating and assisting in the prosecution of violations and provisions of this Ordinance, shall apply to the City Council for authorization to so register and shall be registered with the Office of the Mayor of the City of Hialeah, Florida, following approval by the City Council at a public hearing in accordance with rules and regulations (i.e., criteria) established by the City Council by resolution, and shall thereafter, be empowered to assist in the prosecution of any violation of this Ordinance.

Section 5. Any society or association for the prevention of cruelty to animals registered with the Mayor of the City of Hialeah, Florida, in accordance with the provisions of Section 4 hereinabove, may appoint agents for the purposes of investigating and assisting in the prosecution of violations and provisions of this Ordinance, or any other laws of the City of Hialeah, Florida, for the purpose of protecting animals and preventing any act prohibited hereunder.

Section 6. Repeal of Ordinances in Conflict. All ordinances or parts of ordinances in conflict herewith are hereby repealed to the extent of such conflict.

Section 7. Penalties. Any person, firm or corporation convicted of violating the provisions of this ordinance shall be punished by a fine, not exceeding $500.00, or by a jail sentence, not exceeding sixty (60) days, or both, in the discretion of the Court.

Section 8. Inclusion in Code. The provisions of this Ordinance shall be included and incorporated in the Code of the City of Hialeah, as an addition or amendment thereto, and the sections of this Ordinance shall be re-numbered to conform to the uniform numbering system of the Code.

Section 9. Severability Clause. If any phrase, clause, sentence, paragraph or section of this Ordinance shall be declared invalid or unconstitutional by the judgment or decree of a court of competent jurisdiction, such invalidity or unconstitutionality shall not affect any of the remaining phrases, clauses, sentences, paragraphs or sections of this Ordinance.

Section 10. Effective Date. This Ordinance shall become effective when passed by the City Council of the City of Hialeah and signed by the Mayor of the City of Hialeah.

CITY OF HIALEAH, FLORIDA, ORDINANCE 87-72
(ADOPTED SEPTEMBER 22, 1987)

WHEREAS, the City Council of the City of Hialeah, Florida, has determined that the slaughtering of animals on the premises other than those properly zoned as a slaughter house, is contrary to the public health, safety and welfare of the citizens of Hialeah, Florida.

NOW, THEREFORE, BE IT ORDAINED BY THE MAYOR AND CITY COUNCIL OF THE CITY OF HIALEAH, FLORIDA, that:

Section 1. For the purpose of this Ordinance, the word slaughter shall mean: the killing of animals for food.

Section 2. For the purpose of this Ordinance, the word animal shall mean: any living dumb creature.

Section 3. It shall be unlawful for any person, persons, corporations or associations to slaughter any animal on any premises in the City of Hialeah, Florida, except those properly zoned as a slaughter house, and meeting all the health, safety and sanitation codes prescribed by the City for the operation of a slaughter house.

Section 4. All societies or associations for the prevention of cruelty to animals organized under the laws of the State of Florida, seeking to register with the City of Hialeah for purposes of investigating and assisting in the prosecution of violations and provisions of this Ordinance, shall apply to the City Council for authorization to so register and shall be registered with the Office of the Mayor of the City of Hialeah, Florida, following approval by the City Council at a public hearing in accordance with rules and regulations (i.e., criteria) established by the City Council by resolution, and shall thereafter, be empowered to assist in the prosecution of any violations of this Ordinance.

Section 5. Any society or association for the prevention of cruelty to animals registered with the Mayor of the City of Hialeah, Florida, in accordance with the provisions of Section 4 hereinabove, may appoint agents for the purposes of investigating and assisting in the prosecution of violations and provisions of this Ordinance, or any other laws of the City of Hialeah, Florida, for the purpose of protecting animals and preventing any act prohibited hereunder.

Section 6. This Ordinance shall not apply to any person, group, or organization that slaughters, or processes for sale, small numbers of hogs and/or cattle per week in accordance with an exemption provided by state law.

Section 7. Repeal of Ordinances in Conflict. All ordinances or parts of ordinances in conflict herewith are hereby repealed to the extent of such conflict.

Section 8. Penalties. Any person, firm or corporation convicted of violating the provisions of this ordinance shall be punished by a fine, not exceeding $500.00, or by a jail sentence, not exceeding sixty (60) days, or both, in the discretion of the Court.

Section 9. Inclusion in Code. The provisions of this Ordinance shall be included and incorporated in the Code of the City of Hialeah, as an addition or amendment thereto, and the sections of this Ordinance shall be re-numbered to conform to the uniform numbering system of the Code.

Section 10. Severability Clause. If any phrase, clause, sentence, paragraph or section of this Ordinance shall be declared invalid or unconstitutional by the judgment or decree of a court of competent jurisdiction, such invalidity or unconstitutionality shall not affect any of the remaining phrases, clauses, sentences, paragraphs or sections of this ordinance.

Section 11. Effective Date. This Ordinance shall become effective when passed by the City Council of the City of Hialeah and signed by the Mayor of the City of Hialeah.

GLOSSARY

aleyo: uninitiated devotee

ara orun: "people of the heaven"; Yoruba ancestors or *orishas*

ashe: power, blood, the life force of God, nature, and the universe; the *orishas*

asiento: ceremony of initiation into Santeria in which the *orisha* is seated in the head of the initiated

babalawo: "father of mystery"; an Ifa diviner, a high priest; a male not ordained to his patron divinity but ordained to the order of Ifa

babalosha: "father of/in the *orisha*"; a priest of a specific *orisha* who has ordained others

botanica: retail store specializing in herbs, statues, beads, and other paraphernalia used in Santeria rites and rituals

cabildo: cult associations, social clubs, or chapters; secret societies

Eleda: "owner of the head"; the "guardian angel"

en santo: "in saintliness"; in the way of the saints *(orishas)*

fundamentos: fundamental symbols of the *orishas* — stones, shells, tools — that transmit their *ashe*

Ifa: *orisha* of the oracle, the most sophisticated oracle of the Yoruba and Lukumi priests

ile: house, family, community; the basic units of Lukumi-Santeria worship

Ile-Ife: spiritual capital of Yorubaland; the center of creation

italero: see *oriate*

iyalosha: a female ordained to her patron divinity and who has ordained others

Lukumi: "my friend"; a Yoruba greeting used in Cuba to acknowledge another of Yoruba descent or culture; another name for Santeria

madrina: godmother, priestess of Santeria; used to refer to a devotee's initiator

Mayombe: Congo ethnic group in Cuba; religion derived from Mayombe, often considered sorcery by *santeros*

Negro de nación: African-born Cuban identified with a particular African ethnicity

oba: king; an *oriate*

Obatala: king of white cloth; the *orisha* of creation, wisdom

obi: divination process using coconuts; the personified spirit of the system of divination

ocha: "*orisha*"; often used to refer to Santeria — "*La Ocha*"

odu: An individual divination sign, including proverbs, stories, and sacrifices

{ 169 }

Odudua: *orisha* paired with Obatala, symbolizing totality; the co-creator of Ile-Ife

Olodumare: almighty god, creator of the universe

olorisha: an initiate; one who has the *orisha*

oluwo: highest order of *babalawo*

ori: "head"; the soul or destiny of an individual

oriate: a male or female ordained to his or her patron divinity and a master of *orisha* ordination rites, central teachings, rites of passage, and all major ceremonies; also *oga ogo oriate; oba/italero; akilakua; akakisa*

orisha: divine being, spirit, saint of Santeria

Oya: *orisha* of storms, ruler of the dead

Oyo: Yoruba kingdom at its height in the seventeenth and eighteenth centuries

padrino: godfather, priest of Santeria; used to refer to one's patron and initiator

Palo Monte: the Congo religious tradition in Cuba

Santeria: "the way of the saints"

santero: an initiate of Santeria

santo: "saint," *orisha,* holiness

Shango: *orisha* of thunder, lightning, and force; also, trickster

1959–1960	After the Cuban revolution and Fidel Castro's rise to power, exiles bring Santeria to South Florida, New Jersey, New York, and a few other places.
1961	Ernesto Pichardo, his bother, mother, and stepfather escape Cuba and settle in Little Havana in Miami, Florida.
1970	Ernesto Pichardo is inducted into the Santeria priesthood.
1974	The Church of the Lukumi Babalu Aye is founded by Carmen Pla, Raul Rodriguez, Fernado Pichardo, Ernesto Pichardo, and Gino Negretti.
1978	The first three-day conference of scholars and Catholic Lukumi priests is held under the sponsorship of the Florida Endowment for the Humanities, the University of Miami, and Dr. O. R. Dathorne, director of African American Studies. The first ordination to the patron *orisha* Babalu Aye is performed at the Oyotunji African Village.
1980	The Mariel boatlift brings 125,000 Cubans to South Florida, many of whom had been imprisoned by Castro and were followers of Santeria.
1983–1984	Ernesto Pichardo founds the Institute for New World Studies, with a grant from the Florida Endowment for the Humanities, in order to carry out workshops on Afro-Caribbean religions for law enforcement, hospital, and mental health officials and cultural organizations. Church of the Lukumi Babalu Aye officials and Dade County School Board representatives meet and establish religious exemptions for newly ordained students.
1985	The Church of the Lukumi Babalu Aye offers the first courses on Afro-Caribbean religions at Miami-Dade Community College. Ernesto Pichardo publishes a book on *Oduduwa Obatala* and serves as an adviser on Santeria for the television series *Miami Vice* and the film *The Band of Hand*.

1986	The Church of the Lukumi Babalu Aye initiates its first general campaign to recruit members and officers among senior priests and priestesses in Miami-Dade County.
April 1, 1987	Ernesto Pichardo and others affiliated with the Church of the Lukumi Babalu Aye take possession of a former used-car dealership at 173 West Fifth Street in the city of Hialeah. It is subsequently announced that a church, school, and museum will be established there.
May 21, 1987	Written notice is served to the church that if a certificate of occupancy is not obtained, electricity will be cut off.
May 27–29, 1987	Application for licensing of the church and zoning approval is made.
June 1, 1987	Inspectors visit the property, which fails the fire inspection, electrical inspection, and plumbing inspection.
June 9, 1987	Hialeah's city council adopts Resolution 87-40, incorporating Florida's statute against animal cruelty as an ordinance, and passes Resolution 87-66, expressing concern about religious practices that are inconsistent with "public morals."
July 7–13, 1987	An electrical contractor corrects the church's electrical problems.
July 29, 1987	A plumbing permit is obtained, and an additional bathroom is installed.
August 4, 1987	The property is reinspected and approved, and the church's opening is announced.
August 7, 1987	The church receives its certificate of occupancy.
August 9, 1987	The church sponsors an open house and an Espiritismo mass.
August 11, 1987	Hialeah's city council adopts another resolution expressing opposition to animal sacrifice.
September 8, 1987	Hialeah's city council adopts Ordinance 87-40, prohibiting the possession of animals intended for sacrifice.
September 22, 1987	Hialeah's city council adopts two more ordinances: 87-71 prohibits the ritual sacrifice of animals, and

{ *Animal Sacrifice and Religious Freedom* }

	87-72 prohibits the slaughter of animals on premises not zoned for that purpose.
September 25, 1987	The church files lawsuits against the city council and the city of Hialeah.
December 1987–January 1988	The Church of the Lukumi Babalu Aye relocates to a storefront a few blocks away, at 700 Palm Avenue.
June 10, 1988	Judge Spellman rules that the city council and mayor of Hialeah are immune from liability for allegedly violating the constitutional rights of Ernesto Pichardo and the church.
July–August 1989	A nine-day trial on the constitutional challenge to Hialeah's ordinances is held in Judge Eugene P. Spellman's federal district court.
October 5, 1989	Judge Spellman hands down his decision upholding Hialeah's ordinances against ritual animal sacrifice.
June 11, 1991	A three-judge panel of the Court of Appeals for the Eleventh Circuit upholds Judge Spellman's ruling.
August 21, 1991	A petition for rehearing is denied by the Court of Appeals for the Eleventh Circuit.
November 19, 1991	The church files a petition for certiorari in the Supreme Court.
March 23, 1992	The Supreme Court grants review of the church's case.
November 4, 1992	Oral arguments are heard by the Supreme Court.
June 11, 1993	The Supreme Court hands down its decision, reversing the lower courts and striking down Hialeah's ordinances.
1995	The first group of forty senior priests and priestesses is officially certified as "clergy" by the Church of the Lukumi Babalu Aye.
1997	The Church of the Lukumi Babalu Aye moves to another location on Palm Avenue, one block south of the Hialeah city hall. The first Lukumi marriages are performed. Ernesto Pichardo and the church establish a web site at http://church-of-the-lukumi.org.
1999	The Church of the Lukumi Babalu Aye closes.

RELEVANT CASES

Abington School District v. Schempp, 374 U.S. 203 (1962).

Baker v. Carr, 369 U.S. 186 (1962).

Bob Jones University and Goldsboro Christian School v. United States, 461 U.S. 574 (1983).

Bowen v. Roy, 476 U.S. 693 (1986).

Braunfeld v. Brown, 366 U.S. 599 (1961).

Brown v. Board of Education of Topeka, Kansas, 347 U.S. 483 (1954).

Cantwell v. Connecticut, 310 U.S. 296 (1940).

Chaplinsky v. New Hampshire, 315 U.S. 568 (1942).

Church of the Lukumi Babablu Aye, Inc., and Ernesto Pichardo v. City of Hialeah, 688 F. Supp. 1522 (1988).

Church of the Lukumi Babablu Aye, Inc., and Ernesto Pichardo v. City of Hialeah, 723 F. Supp. 1467 (1989).

Church of the Lukumi Babablu Aye, Inc., and Ernesto Pichardo v. City of Hialeah, 936 F. 2d 586 (1991).

Church of the Lukumi Babablu Aye, Inc., and Ernesto Pichardo v. City of Hialeah, 508 U.S. 520 (1993).

City of Boerne v. Flores, 521 U.S. 507 (1997).

Cruz v. Beto, 405 U.S. 319 (1972).

Davis v. Beason, 133 U.S. 333 (1890).

Douglas v. City of Jeanette, 319 U.S. 157 (1943).

Dred Scott v. Sandford, 60 U.S. 39 (1857).

Employment Division, Department of Human Resources of Oregon v. Smith (Smith I), 485 U.S. 660 (1988).

Employment Division, Department of Human Resources of Oregon v. Smith (Smith II), 494 U.S. 872 (1990).

Engel v. Vitale, 370 U.S. 421 (1962).

Everson v. Board of Education of Ewing Township, 330 U.S. 1 (1947).

First Church of Chango, Inc. v. American Society for Prevention of Cruelty to Animals, 134 A.D. 2d 971 (1987), *appeal denied*, 70 N.Y. 2d 616 (1988).

Frazee v. Illinois Department of Employment Security, 489 U.S. 829 (1989).

Gallagher v. Crown Kosher Super Market, Inc., 366 U.S. 617 (1961).

Garber v. Kansas, 389 U.S. 51 (1967).

Gertz v. Robert Welch, Inc., 418 U.S. 323 (1974).

Gideon v. Wainwright, 372 U.S. 335 (1963).

Goldman v. Winberger, 475 U.S. 503 (1986).

Hamilton v. Regents of the University of California, 293 U.S. 245 (1934).

Heffron v. International Society for Krishna Consciousness, 452 U.S. 640 (1981).

Hernandez v. Commissioner of Internal Revenue, 490 U.S. 680 (1989).

Hobbie v. Unemployment Appeals Commission of Florida, 480 U.S. 136 (1987).

International Society for Krishna Consciousness v. Lee, 505 U.S. 830 (1992).

Jamison v. Texas, 318 U.S. 413 (1943).

Jimmy Swaggart Ministries v. Board of Equalization of California, 493 U.S. 378 (1990).

Jones v. Opelika, 316 U.S. 584 (1942).

Lamb's Chapel v. Center Moriches Union Free School District, 508 U.S. 384 (1993).

Late Corporation of Church of Jesus Christ of Latter Day Saints v. United States, 136 U.S. 1 (1890).

Lee v. Weisman, 505 U.S. 577 (1992).

Lemon v. Kurtzman, 403 U.S. 602 (1971).

Lovell v. City of Griffin, 303 U.S. 444 (1938).

Lyng v. Northwest Indian Cemetery Protective Association, 485 U.S. 439 (1988).

Mapp v. Ohio, 367 U.S. 643 (1961).

Marsh v. Alabama, 326 U.S. 501 (1946).

Martin v. Struthers, 319 U.S. 141 (1943).

McDaniel v. Paty, 435 U.S. 618 (1978).

McGowan v. State of Maryland, 366 U.S. 420 (1961).

Minersville School District v. Gobitis, 310 U.S. 586 (1940).

Minnesota v. Hershberger, 495 U.S. 901 (1990).

Miranda v. Arizona, 384 U.S. 436 (1966).

Murdock v. Commonwealth of Pennsylvania, 319 U.S. 105 (1943).

Murphy v. Ramsey, 114 U.S. 15 (1885).

Murray v. Curlett, 374 U.S. 203 (1963).

Niemotko v. Maryland, 340 U.S. 268 (1951).

O'Lone v. Shabazz, 482 U.S. 342 (1987).

Planned Parenthood of Southeastern Pennsylvania v. Casey, 505 U.S. 833 (1992).

Prince v. Massachusetts, 321 U.S. 158 (1944).

Regents of the University of California, Davis v. Bakke, 438 U.S. 265 (1978).

Reynolds v. United States, 98 U.S. 145 (1878).

Roe v. Wade, 410 U.S. 113 (1973).

Schneider v. New Jersey, 308 U.S. 147 (1939).

Sherbert v. Verner, 374 U.S. 398 (1963).

State v. Massey, 229 N.C. 734 (1949).

Thomas v. Review Board of Indiana, 450 U.S. 707 (1981).

Tony and Susan Alamo Foundation v. Secretary of Labor, 471 U.S. 290 (1985).

Torcaso v. Watkins, 367 U.S. 488 (1961).

Two-Guys from Harrison-Allentown, Inc. v. McGinley, 366 U.S. 582 (1961).

United States v. Ballard, 322 U.S. 78 (1944).

United States v. Lee, 455 U.S. 252 (1982).

United States v. Seeger, 380 U.S. 163 (1965).

Webster v. Reproductive Health Services, 492 U.S. 490 (1989).

Welsh v. United States, 398 U.S. 333 (1970).

West Virginia State Board of Education v. Barnette, 319 U.S. 624 (1943).

Wisconsin v. Yoder, 406 U.S. 208 (1972).

Wooley v. Maynard, 430 U.S. 705 (1977).

Zobrest v. Catalina Foothills School District, 509 U.S. 1 (1993).

BIBLIOGRAPHIC ESSAY

There are countless articles on the history and legal theory of the First Amendment guarantees of religious freedom, along with examinations of court decisions bearing on them. They can be found in law reviews and journals of history, religion, and political science. They are omitted here because they are too numerous and can easily be located through the *Index to Legal Periodicals*, the *Social Science Index*, *Lexis*, and other references. This essay is confined to the leading books on topics related to the Supreme Court's decision in *Church of the Lukumi Babalu Aye v. City of Hialeah*. Most of these books include notes and bibliographies that will lead the reader to additional literature in periodicals.

For explanations of the history and religious traditions of the Yoruba people, see J. O. Awolalu, *Yoruba Beliefs and Sacrificial Rites* (London: Longmans, 1979); the widely cited scholarly works by William R. Bascom, *Ifa Divination: Communication between Gods and Men in West Africa* (Bloomington: Indiana University Press, 1969), *The Yoruba of Southwestern Nigeria* (Bloomington: Indiana University Press, 1969), and *Sixteen Cowries: Yoruba Divination from Africa to the New World* (Bloomington: Indiana University Press, 1980); and Judith Gleason, *Orisha: The Gods of Yorubaland* (New York: Atheneum, 1971), and *A Recitation of Ifa, Oracle of the Yoruba* (New York: Grossman, 1973). Also of interest is Carl M. Hunt, *Oyotunji Village: The Yoruba Movement in America* (Washington, D.C.: University Press of America, 1979).

For background on Cuba, see Jane Franklin, *The Cuban Revolution and the United States: A Chronological History* (New York: Ocean Press and the Center for Cuban Studies, 1992); K. S. Karol, *Guerrillas in Power: The Course of the Cuban Revolution* (New York: Hill and Wang, 1970); Louis A. Perez Jr., *Cuba: Between Reform and Revolution* (New York: Oxford University Press, 1988); and Wayne S. Smith, *Portrait of Cuba* (Atlanta: Turner Publications, 1991).

In the past few decades, numerous books have appeared on Santeria, many of which tend to be sensational and often misleading. Two of the most scholarly and recommended books, linking the Yoruba religious tradition with Santeria in Cuba and the United States, are George Brandon, *Santeria from Africa to the New World: The Dead Sell Memories* (Bloomington: Indiana University Press, 1993), and Joseph M. Murphy, *Santeria: African Spirits in America* (Boston: Beacon Press, 1993). From a comparative perspective, Joseph M. Murphy's *Working the Spirit: Ceremonies of the African Diaspora* (Boston: Beacon Press, 1994) is a useful introduction to how African religious practices were transplanted and transformed in Brazil, Cuba, Haiti, Jamaica, and the United States. Also useful is William R. Bascom, *Shango in the New World* (Austin: University of Texas, African and Afro-American Research Institute, 1972); Gary Edwards and John Mason, *Black Gods: Orisa Studies in the New*

World (New York: Yoruba Theological Archministry, 1985); and Judith Gleason, *Santeria, Bronx* (New York: Atheneum, 1975).

For detailed discussions of the myths and rites of Santeria, see the inelegantly translated but still useful book by a Miami Cuban-American priest of Santeria, Julio Garcia Cortez: *The Osha: Secrets of the Yoruba-Lucumi-Santeria Religion in the United States and the Americas* (Brooklyn: Athelia Henrietta Press, 2000). See also Ernesto Pichardo and Lourdes Nieto, *Oduduwa Obatala* (Miami: Church of the Lukumi Babalu Aye, 1984); and Wande Abimbola, *Ifa Will Mend Our Broken World: Thought on Yoruba Religion and Culture in Africa and the Diaspora*, with interviews and introduction by Ivor Miller (Roxbury, Mass.: AIM Books, 1997). Marta Moreno Vega's *The Altar of My Soul: The Living Traditions of Santeria* (New York: Ballantine, 2000) recounts the experiences of a college professor and follower of Santeria. For a different perspective and more sensational discussions of the rites and rituals of Santeria, see the works of Migene Gonzales-Wippler: *Santeria: African Magic in Latin America* (Garden City, N.Y.: Doubleday/Anchor, 1973); *The Santeria Experience* (Englewood Cliffs, N.J.: Prentice-Hall, 1982); *Rituals and Spells of Santeria* (New York: Original Publications, 1984); and *Tales of the Orishas* (New York: Original Publications, 1985).

There are numerous examinations of the history and legal theories of the First Amendment's freedom of religion clauses. Among the classic scholarly works are Mark DeWolfe Howe, *The Garden and the Wilderness: Religion and Government in American Constitutional History* (Chicago: University of Chicago Press, 1965); Leonard W. Levy, *The Establishment Clause: Religion and the First Amendment* (New York: Macmillan, 1986); Dallin Oaks, ed., *The Wall between Church and State* (Chicago: University of Chicago Press, 1963); and Philip Hamburger, *Separation of Church and State* (Cambridge: Harvard University Press, 2002). Also useful on the history of religious freedom is Thomas Curry's *The First Freedoms: Church and State in America to the Passage of the First Amendment* (New York: Oxford University Press, 1986).

No less scholarly and written from the perspective of a lawyer involved in many of the early cases decided by the Supreme Court are Leo Pfeffer's *Church, State, and Freedom* (Boston: Beacon Press, 1967) and *God, Caesar and the Constitution* (Boston: Beacon Press, 1975), as well as Anson Stokes and Leo Pfeffer, *Church and State in the United States* (New York: Harper and Row, 1965). Excerpts of the principal cases decided by the Supreme Court can be found in, among other casebooks, David M. O'Brien, *Constitutional Law and Politics: Civil Rights and Civil Liberties*, 5th ed. (New York: W. W. Norton, 2003). See also John T. Noonan, John Noonan Jr., and Edward M. Gaffney, eds., *Religious Freedom: History, Cases, and Other Materials on the Interaction of Religion and Government* (Mineola, N.Y.: Foundation Press, 2001).

For competing views of religion and law in the United States in the 1980s and 1990s, see and compare James Davidson Hunter, *Culture Wars: The Struggle to Define America* (New York: Basic Books, 1991), and Stephen L. Carter, *The Culture of Disbelief: How American Law and Politics Trivialize Religious Devotion* (New York: Basic Books, 1993). Also useful is historian Leonard Levy's *Blasphemy* (New York: Alfred A. Knopf, 1993); Mary C. Segers and Ted G. Jelen, *A Wall of Separation? Debating the Public Role of Religion* (Lanham, Md.: Rowman and Littlefield, 1998); Mark A. Noll, ed., *Religion and America Politics: From the Colonial Period to the Present* (New York: Oxford University Press, 1990); Ted G. Jelen and Clyde Wilcox, *Public Attitudes toward Church and State* (Armonk, N.Y.: M. E. Sharpe, 1995); Gary Wills, *Under God: Religion and American Politics* (New York: Simon and Schuster, 1990); Harold Bloom, *The American Religion: The Emergence of the Post-Christian Nation* (New York: Simon and Schuster, 1992); Kenneth D. Wald, *Religion and Politics in the United States*, 3rd ed. (Washington, D.C.: CQ Press, 1996); and John Witte Jr., *Religion and American Constitutional Experiment* (Boulder, Colo.: Westview Press, 1999).

Works specifically devoted to the First Amendment's free exercise clause include Louis Fisher, *Religious Liberty in America: Political Safeguards* (Lawrence: University Press of Kansas, 2002); Bette Novit Evans, *Interpreting the Free Exercise of Religion: The Constitution and American Pluralism* (Chapel Hill: University of North Carolina Press, 1997); and Catherine Cookson, *Regulating Religion: The Courts and the Free Exercise Clause* (New York: Oxford University Press, 2001). See also, more generally, John T. Noonan, *The Lustre of Our Country: The American Experience of Religious Freedom* (Berkeley: University of California Press, 1998), and *Religion, State and the Burger Court* (New York: Prometheus Books, 1985); Francis Graham Lee, ed., *All Imaginable Liberty: The Religious Clauses of the First Amendment* (Lanham, Md.: University Press of America, 1995); Winnifred Fallers Sullivan, *Paying the Words Extra: Religious Discourse in the Supreme Court of the United States* (Cambridge: Harvard University Press, 1965); Jesse Choper, *Securing Religious Liberty: Principles for Judicial Interpretation of the Religion Clauses* (Chicago: University of Chicago Press, 1995); and Michael J. Perry, *Love and Power: The Role of Religion and Morality in American Politics* (New York: Oxford University Press, 1991).

For conservative scholarly criticisms of the Court's interpretation of the First Amendment's free exercise clause, see Walter Berns, *The First Amendment and American Democracy* (New York: Basic Books, 1976), and Michael Malbin, *Religion and Politics: The Intentions of the Authors of the First Amendment* (Washington, D.C.: American Enterprise Institute, 1978). For criticisms of such conservative critics, see Isaac Kramnick and Laurence Moore, *The Godless Constitution: The Case against Religious Correctness* (New York: W. W. Norton, 1996). For other provocative criticism of the Supreme Court's rulings, see Steven Smith, *Foreordained Failure: The Quest for a Constitutional Principle of Religious Freedom* (New York: Oxford University Press, 1995).

There are several interesting and informative books on specific controversies over the free exercise of religion and particular decisions, including David Manwaring's *Render unto Caesar: The Flag Salute Controversy* (Chicago: University of Chicago Press, 1962); Leonard A. Stevens, *Salute! The Case of the Bible vs. the Flag* (New York: Coward, McCann and Goeghegan, 1973); and R. Laurence Moore, *Religious Outsiders and the Making of Americans* (New York: Oxford University Press, 1986). The authoritative study of the controversy surrounding the ruling in *Oregon v. Smith* is Carolyn N. Long's *Religious Freedom and Indian Rights: The Case of* Oregon v. Smith (Lawrence: University Press of Kansas, 2000), but see also Garrett Epps's no less rewarding book *To an Unknown God: Religious Freedom on Trial* (New York: St. Martin's Press, 2001). For another excellent study of a landmark case, see Edward Larson's award-winning *Summer for the Gods: The Scopes Trial and America's Continuing Debate over Science and Religion* (New York: Basic Books, 1997).

A number of books have focused on the litigants and interest groups involved in litigating free exercise controversies. A good overview of the crucial role of the Jehovah's Witnesses in bringing early free exercise claims to the Supreme Court is Shawn Francis Peters's *Judging the Jehovah's Witnesses: Religious Persecution and the Dawn of the Rights Revolution* (Lawrence: University Press of Kansas, 2002). See also M. James Penton, *Apocalypse Delayed: The Story of the Jehovah's Witnesses*, 2nd ed. (Toronto: University of Toronto, 1997); Merlin O. Newton, *Armed with the Constitution: Jehovah's Witnesses in Alabama and the U.S. Supreme Court* (Tuscaloosa: University of Alabama Press, 1995); Edwin B. Firmage and Richard C. Mangrum, *Zion in the Courts: A Legal History of the Church of Jesus Christ of Latter-Day Saints, 1830–1900* (Urbana: University of Illinois Press, 1988); Gregg Ivers, *To Build a Wall: American Jews and the Separation of Church and State* (Charlottesville: University Press of Virginia, 1995); Clyde Wilcox, *Onward, Christian Soldiers? The Religious Right in American Politics* (Boulder, Colo.: Westview Press, 1996); Kathleen M. Moore, *Al-Mughtaribun: American Law and the Transformation of Muslim Life in the United States* (Albany: State University of New York Press, 1995); and Steven P. Brown, *Trumping Religion: The New Christian Right, the Free Speech Clause, and the Courts* (Tuscaloosa: University of Alabama Press, 2002). See also Peter Irons, *The Courage of Their Convictions* (New York: Free Press, 1988).

On interest-group litigation before the Court more generally, see Clement Vose, *Caucasians Only: The Supreme Court, the NAACP and the Restrictive Covenant Cases* (Berkeley: University of California Press, 1959); Mark Tushnet, *The NAACP's Legal Strategy against Segregated Education, 1925–1950* (Chapel Hill: University of North Carolina Press, 1987); Lee Epstein, *Conservatives in Court* (Knoxville: University of Tennessee Press, 1985); Karen O'Connor, *Women's Organizations' Use of the Court* (Lexington, Mass.: Lexington Books, 1980); Kevin McGuire, *The Supreme Court Bar: Legal Elites in the Washington*

Community (Charlottesville: University Press of Virginia, 1993); Gerald Rosenberg, *The Hollow Hope: Can Courts Bring about Social Change?* (Chicago: University of Chicago Press, 1991); Samuel Walker, *In Defense of American Liberties: A History of the ACLU* (New York: Oxford University Press, 1990); and Jack Greenberg, *Crusaders in the Courts* (New York: Basic Books, 1994).

The growing literature on the rights of animals and the animal rights movement deserves mentioning. Peter Singer's *Animal Liberation: A New Ethics for Our Treatment of Animals* (first issued by Random House in 1975 and reissued as a second edition in 1990), has been called the bible of the animal rights movement. A bioethics philosopher, Singer is known for grounding animal rights in utilitarian arguments. See also his *In Defense of Animals* (Oxford: Basil Blackwell, 1985) and *Practical Ethics* (Cambridge: Cambridge University Press, 1993). For his personal reflections on the contemporary origins of the animal rights movement, see Peter Singer, *Ethics into Action: Henry Spira and the Animal Rights Movement* (Lanham, Md.: Rowman and Littlefield, 2000). Another influential philosopher, Tom Regan, is known for staking out a more extreme, absolutist moral position based on nonviolence and vegetarianism, particularly with respect to the immorality of animal experimentation. His books include *The Case for Animal Rights* (Berkeley: University of California Press, 1985), *Animal Sacrifices: Religious Perspectives on the Use of Animals in Science* (Philadelphia: Temple University Press, 1986), *The Struggle for Animal Rights* (Clarks Summit, Pa.: International Society for Animal Rights, 1987), and *Defending Animal Rights* (Chicago: University of Illinois Press, 2001). Finally, Steven M. Wise makes the case for animal rights based on the common DNA of animals and humans in *Drawing the Line: Science and the Case for Animal Rights* (New York: Perseus Press, 2002); see also his *Rattling the Cage: Toward Legal Rights for Animals* (New York: Perseus Press, 2001). Of related interest is Jonathan Marks's *What It Means to Be 98 Percent Chimpanzee: Apes, People, and the Genes* (Berkeley: University of California Press, 2002).

A number of books examine the emergence of forces that shaped the animal rights movement, focusing on incidents and individuals who helped make it into a political and social movement, as well as on the development of its legal arguments and litigation strategies. Among them are Kathy Snow Guillermo, *Monkey Business: The Disturbing Case That Launched the Animal Rights Movement (People for the Ethical Treatment of Animals)* (New York: National Press Books, 1993); James M. Jasper and Dorothy Nelkin, *The Animal Rights Crusade: The Growth of a Moral Protest* (New York: Free Press, 1991); Harold D. Guither, *Animal Rights: History and Scope of a Radical Social Movement* (Carbondale: Southern Illinois University Press, 1998); Helena Silverstein, *Unleashing Rights: Law, Meaning, and the Animal Rights Movement* (Ann Arbor: University of Michigan Press, 1996); and Gary L. Francione,

Rain without Thunder: The Ideology of the Animal Rights Movement (Philadelphia: Temple University Press, 1996).

Finally, for further discussion of the operation and work of the Supreme Court, see David M. O'Brien, *Storm Center: The Supreme Court in American Politics*, 6th ed. (New York: W. W. Norton, 2003), an institutional history of the Supreme Court. Other useful works include Henry J. Abraham, *The Judicial Process*, 7th ed. (New York: Oxford University Press, 1998); Cornell Clayton and Howard Gillman, eds., *Supreme Court Decision Making: New Institutionalist Approaches* (Chicago: University of Chicago Press, 1999); Robert G. McCloskey, revised by Stanford Levinson, *The American Supreme Court* (Chicago: University of Chicago Press, 2001); and David M. O'Brien, ed., *Judges on Judging: Views from the Bench*, 2nd ed. (Washington, D.C.: Congressional Quarterly Press, 2004). For a useful reference and collection of data on the Supreme Court, see Lee Epstein, Jeffrey Segal, Harold Spaeth, and Thomas Walker, eds., *The Supreme Court Compendium: Data, Decisions and Developments*, 2nd ed. (Washington, D.C.: Congressional Quarterly Press, 2001).

Fox, Michael, 83–85, 93
Frank, Judge Jerome, 76
Frankel, Judge Marvin, 76
Frankfurter, Justice Felix, 59, 117, 152
Frazee v. Illinois Department of Employment Security, 66
Freedom of religious belief, x, 16, 26, 103, 110
   vs. animal rights, 38, 105
   and immigrants, 50
   Pichardo espousing, 26
   Rehnquist Court on, 97
   Spellman's argument, 91
   victory for, 152
Freedom of worship, ix, x, 35
Free exercise clause, ix, 51, 53, 54, 56, 66, 69, 104, 106, 110, 114
   Kennedy on, 140, 145, 159
   Rehnquist Court on, 70
   rulings on, 55, 58
   Rutherford Institute on, 106
   Souter on, 146–147
   Spellman on, 93

Garbage, 85–86, 126, 134, 144. *See also* Carcasses, animal
Garber v. Kansas, 67
Garrett, Richard G., 48, 56, 73
   arguing before Eleventh Circuit, 96
   arguing before Spellman, 76, 77, 85, 86
   briefs filed in Rehnquist Court, 111–115
   oral arguments before U.S. Supreme Court, 125–134 134, 141, 143
Garvey, Marcus, 24
General Assembly of the Presbyterian Church, 102

General Conference of Seventh-day Adventists, 94, 102
Gertz v. Robert Welch, 50
Gideon v. Wainwright, 64
Ginsburg, Justice Ruth Bader, 158
Gobitis. See Minersville School District v. Gobitis
Goldman v. Weinberger, 67–68
Goldsmith, Stephen M., 111
Gonzalez, Irma, 150
Gonzales-Wippler, Migene, 30–31, 85
Gross, Richard, 43, 44, 134

Hamilton v. Regents of the University of California, 59
Harlem, 24
Harm to children. *See* Children, harm to
Harassment, 47, 49, 76–77, 88
   Spellman's ruling on, 91
Health risks, human, 125, 144
Heffron v. International Society for Krishna Consciousness, 56
Henderson, Judge Albert J., 96
Hendrix, Joli, 87–88
Henry, Patrick, 52
Hernandez v. Commissioner of Internal Revenue, 70
Hialeah, city of, x
   allows church to open, 42
   corrupt politics of, ix
   Duarte's response to Spellman, 89–90
   resolutions and ordinances, 34, 77, 83–88
   settlement agreement, 160
   Spellman's ruling on ordinances in, 90–93
Hialeah city council, 36
   public meetings, 42–44, 45
   See also Ordinances; Resolutions